THE SOCIAL HISTORY
OF SMOKING

G.L. APPERSON, I.S.O.

Contents

PREFACE 7

I THE FIRST PIPES OF TOBACCO SMOKED IN ENGLAND...................9

II TOBACCO TRIUMPHANT: SMOKING FASHIONABLE ....
    AND UNIVERSAL..18

III TOBACCO TRIUMPHANT (continued) --SELLERS OF ....
    TOBACCO AND PROFESSORS OF SMOKING--............................
    ABUSE AND PRAISE OF TOBACCO 28

IV CAVALIER AND ROUNDHEAD SMOKERS 40

V SMOKING IN THE RESTORATION PERIOD 48

VI SMOKING UNDER KING WILLIAM III AND QUEEN ANNE 58

VII SMOKING UNFASHIONABLE: EARLY GEORGIAN DAYS............68

VIII SMOKING UNFASHIONABLE (continued):.....................................
    LATER GEORGIAN DAYS 82

IX SIGNS OF REVIVAL 94

X EARLY VICTORIAN DAYS...107

XI LATER VICTORIAN DAYS...122

XII SMOKING IN THE TWENTIETH CENTURY 132

XIII SMOKING BY WOMEN 140

XIV SMOKING IN CHURCH 153

XV TOBACCONISTS' SIGNS...159

THE SOCIAL HISTORY
OF SMOKING

BY

G.L. APPERSON, I.S.O.

TO
J.H.M. AND R.W.B.
GOOD FRIENDS AND
GOOD SMOKERS
BOTH

PREFACE

This is the first attempt to write the history of smoking in this country from the social point of view. There have been many books written about tobacco--F.W. Fairholt's "History of Tobacco," 1859, and the "Tobacco" (1857) of Andrew Steinmetz, are still valuable authorities--but hitherto no one has told the story of the fluctuations of fashion in respect of the practice of smoking.

Much that is fully and well treated in such a work as Fairholt's "History" is ignored in the following pages. I have tried to confine myself strictly to the changes in the attitude of society towards smoking, and to such historical and social side-lights as serve to illuminate that theme.

The tobacco-pipe was popular among every section of society in this country in an amazingly short space of time after smoking was first practised for pleasure, and retained its ascendancy for no inconsiderable period. Signs of decline are to be observed during the latter part of the seventeenth century; and in the course of its successor smoking fell more and more under the ban of fashion. Early in the nineteenth century tobacco-smoking had reached its nadir from the social point of view. Then came the introduction of the cigar and the revival of smoking in the circles from which it had long been almost entirely absent. The practice was hedged about and obstructed by a host of restrictions and conventions, but as the nineteenth century advanced the triumphant progress of tobacco became more and more marked. The introduction of the cigarette completed what the cigar had begun; barriers and prejudices crumbled and disappeared with increasing rapidity; until at the present day tobacco-smoking in England--by pipe or cigar or cigarette--is more general, more continuous, and more free from conventional restrictions than at any period since the early days of its triumph in the first decades of the seventeenth century.

The tracing and recording of this social history of the smoking-habit, touching as it does so many interesting points and details of domestic manners and customs, has been a task of peculiar pleasure. To me it has been a labour of love; but no one can be more conscious of the many imperfections of these pages than I am.

I should like to add that I am indebted to Mr. Vernon Rendall, editor of The Athenaeum, for a number of valuable references and suggestions.

G.L.A.

HAYWARDS HEATH.   September 1914.

I

THE FIRST PIPES OF TOBACCO SMOKED IN ENGLAND

Before the wine of sunny Rhine, or even Madam Clicquot's,
Let all men praise, with loud hurras, this panacea of Nicot's.
The debt confess, though none the less they love the grape and barley,
Which Frenchmen owe to good Nicot, and Englishmen to Raleigh.
  DEAN HOLE.

There is little doubt that the smoke of herbs and leaves of various kinds was inhaled in this country, and in Europe generally, long before tobacco was ever heard of on this side the Atlantic. But whatever smoking of this kind took place was medicinal and not social. Many instances have been recorded of the finding of pipes resembling those used for tobacco-smoking in Elizabethan times, in positions and in circumstances which would seem to point to much greater antiquity of use than the form of the pipes supports; but some at least of these finds will not bear the interpretation which has been put upon them, and in other cases the presence of pipes could reasonably be accounted for otherwise than by associating them with the antiquity claimed for them. In any case, the entire absence of any allusions whatever to smoking in any shape or form in our pre-Elizabethan literature, or in mediaeval or earlier art, is sufficient proof that from the social point of view smoking did not then exist. The inhaling of the smoke of dried herbs for medicinal purposes, whether through a pipe-shaped funnel or otherwise, had nothing in it akin to the smoking of tobacco for both individual and social pleasure, and therefore lies outside the scope of this book.

It may further be added that though the use of tobacco was known and practised on the continent of Europe for some time before smoking became common in
England--it was taken to Spain from Mexico by a physician about 1560, and Jean
Nicot about the same time sent tobacco seeds to France--yet such use was exclusively for medicinal purposes. The smoking of tobacco in England seems from the
first to have been much more a matter of pleasure than of hygiene.

Who first smoked a pipe of tobacco in England? The honour is divided among
several claimants. It has often been stated that Captain William Middleton or My-
ddelton (son of Richard Middleton, Governor of Denbigh Castle), a Captain Price
and a Captain Koet were the first who smoked publicly in London, and that folk
flocked from all parts to see them; and it is usually added that pipes were not then
invented, so they smoked the twisted leaf, or cigars. This account first appeared
in one of the volumes of Pennant's "Tour in Wales." But the late Professor Arber
long ago pointed out that the remark as to the mode of smoking by cigars and not
by pipes was simply Pennant's speculation. The authority for the rest of the story is
a paper in the Sebright MSS., which, in an account of William Middleton, has the
remark: "It is sayed, that he, with Captain Thomas Price of Plasyollin and one Captain Koet, were the first who smoked, or (as they called it) drank tobacco publickly
in London; and that the Londoners flocked from all parts to see them." No date is
named, and no further particulars are available.

Another Elizabethan who is often said to have smoked the first pipe in England
is Ralph Lane, the first Governor of Virginia, who came home with Drake in 1586.
Lane is said to have given Sir Walter Raleigh an Indian pipe and to have shown him
how to use it. There is no original authority, however, for the statement that Lane
first smoked tobacco in England, and, moreover, he was not the first English visitor
to Virginia to return to this country. One Captain Philip Amadas accompanied Captain Barlow, who commanded on the occasion of Raleigh's first voyage of discovery,
when the country was formally taken possession of and named Virginia in honour
of Queen Elizabeth. This was early in 1584. The two captains reached England
in September 1584, bringing with them the natives of whom King James I, in his
"Counter-blaste to Tobacco," speaks as "some two or three Savage men," who "were
brought in, together with this Savage custome," i.e. of smoking. It is extremely
improbable that Captains Amadas and Barlow, when reporting to Raleigh on their

expedition, did not also make him acquainted with the Indian practice of smoking. This would be two years before the return of Ralph Lane.

But certainly pipes were smoked in England before 1584. The plant was introduced into Europe, as we have seen, about 1560, and it was under cultivation in England by 1570. In the 1631 edition of Stow's "Chronicles" it is stated that tobacco was "first brought and made known by Sir John Hawkins, about the year 1565, but not used by Englishmen in many years after." There is only one reference to tobacco in Hawkins's description of his travels. In the account of his second voyage (1564-65) he says: "The Floridians when they travel have a kinde of herbe dryed, which with a cane, and an earthen cup in the end, with fire, and the dried herbs put together do smoke thoro the cane the smoke thereof, which smoke satisfieth their hunger, and therewith they live foure or five days without meat or drinke." Smoking was thus certainly known to Hawkins in 1565, but much reliance cannot be placed on the statement in the Stow of 1631 that he first made known the practice in this country, because that statement appears in no earlier edition of the "Chronicles." Moreover, as opposed to the allegation that tobacco was "not used by Englishmen in many years after" 1565, there is the remark by William Harrison, in his "Chronologie," 1588, that in 1573 "the taking in of the smoke of the Indian herbe called Tobacco, by an instrument formed like a little ladell, whereby it passeth from the mouth into the head and stomach, is gretlie taken up and used in England." The "little ladell" describes the early form of the tobacco-pipe, with small and very shallow bowl.

King James, in his reference to the "first Author" of what he calls "this abuse," clearly had Sir Walter Raleigh in view, and it is Raleigh with whom in the popular mind the first pipe of tobacco smoked in England is usually associated. The tradition is crystallized in the story of the schoolboy who, being asked "What do you know about Sir Walter Raleigh?" replied: "Sir Walter Raleigh introduced tobacco into England, and when smoking it in this country said to his servant, 'Master Ridley, we are to-day lighting a candle in England which by God's blessing will never be put out'"!

The truth probably is that whoever actually smoked the first pipe, it was Raleigh who brought the practice into common use. It is highly probable, also, that Raleigh was initiated in the art of smoking by Thomas Hariot. This was made clear, I think, by the late Dr. Brushfield in the second of the valuable papers on matters connected with the life and achievements of Sir Walter, which he contributed under the title of "Raleghana" to the "Transactions" of the Devonshire Association. Hariot was sent out by Raleigh for the specific purpose of inquiring into and reporting upon the natural productions of Virginia. He returned in 1586, and in 1588 published the results of his researches in a thin quarto with an extremely long-winded title beginning "A briefe and true report of the new found land of Virginia" and continuing for a further 138 words.

In this "Report" Hariot says of the tobacco plant: "There is an herbe which is sowed a part by itselfe and is called by the inhabitants Vppowoc: In the West Indies it hath divers names, according to the severall places and countries where it groweth and is used: The Spaniardes generally call it Tobacco. The leaves thereof being dried and brought into powder: they use to take the fume or smoke thereof by sucking it through pipes made of claie into their stomacke and heade: from whence it purgeth superfluous fleame and other grosse humors, openeth all the pores and passages of the body: by which meanes the use thereof, not only preserveth the body from obstructions: but if also any be, so that they have not beane of too long continuance, in short time breaketh them: wherby their bodies are notably preserved in health, and know not many greevous diseases wherewithall wee in England are oftentimes afflicted."

So far Hariot's "Report" regarded tobacco from the medicinal point of view only; but it is important to note that he goes on to describe his personal experience of the practice of smoking in words that suggest the pleasurable nature of the experience. He says: "We ourselves during the time we were there used to suck it after their maner, as also since our returne, and have found maine [? manie] rare and wonderful experiments of the vertues thereof: of which the relation woulde require a volume by itselfe: the use of it by so manie of late, men and women of great calling as else, and some learned Physitians also, is sufficient witness."

Who can doubt that Hariot, in reporting direct to Sir Walter Raleigh, showed his employer how "to suck it after their maner"?

All the evidence agrees that whoever taught Raleigh, it was Raleigh's example that brought smoking into notice and common use. Long before his death in 1618 it had become fashionable, as we shall see, in all ranks of society. He is said to have smoked a pipe on the morning of his execution, before he went to the scaffold, a tradition which is quite credible.

Every one knows the legend of the water (or beer) thrown over Sir Walter by his servant when he first saw his master smoking, and imagined he was on fire. The story was first associated with Raleigh by a writer in 1708 in a magazine called the British Apollo. According to this yarn Sir Walter usually "indulged himself in Smoaking secretly, two pipes a Day; at which time, he order'd a Simple Fellow, who waited, to bring him up a Tankard of old Ale and Nutmeg, always laying aside the Pipe, when he heard his servant coming." On this particular occasion, however, the pipe was not laid aside in time, and the "Simple Fellow," imagining his master was on fire, as he saw the smoke issuing from his mouth, promptly put the fire out by sousing him with the contents of the tankard. One difficulty about this story is the alleged secrecy of Raleigh's indulgence in tobacco. There seems to be no imaginable reason why he should not have smoked openly. Later versions turn the ale into water and otherwise vary the story.

But the story was a stock jest long before it was associated with Raleigh. The earliest example of it occurs in the "Jests" attributed to Richard Tarleton, the famous comic performer of the Elizabethan stage, who died in 1588--the year of the Armada. "Tarlton's Jests" appeared in 1611, and the story in question, which is headed "How Tarlton tooke tobacco at the first comming up of it," runs as follows:

"Tarlton, as other gentlemen used, at the first comming up of tobacco, did take it more for fashion's sake than otherwise, and being in a roome, set between two men overcome with wine, and they never seeing the like, wondered at it, and seeing the vapour come out of Tarlton's nose, cryed out, fire, fire, and threw a cup of wine in Tarlton's face. Make no more stirre, quoth Tarlton, the fire is quenched: if the sheriffes come, it will turne to a fine, as the custome is. And drinking that againe, fie, sayes the other, what a stinke it makes; I am almost poysoned. If it offend, saies Tarlton, let every one take a little of the smell, and so the savour will quickly goe: but tobacco whiffes made them leave him to pay all."

In the early days of smoking, the smoker was very generally said to "drink" tobacco.

Another early example of the story occurs in Barnaby Rich's "Irish Hubbub," 1619, where a "certain Welchman coming newly to London," and for the first time seeing a man smoking, extinguished the fire with a "bowle of beere" which he had in his hand.

Various places are traditionally associated with Raleigh's first pipe. The most surprising claim, perhaps, is that of Penzance, for which there is really no evidence at all. Miss Courtney, writing in the Folk-Lore Journal, 1887, says: "There is a myth that Sir Walter Raleigh landed at Penzance Quay when he returned from Virginia, and on it smoked the first tobacco ever seen in England, but for this I do not believe that there is the slightest foundation. Several western ports, both in Devon and Cornwall, make the same boast." Miss Courtney might have added that Sir Walter never himself visited Virginia at all.

Another place making a similar claim is Hemstridge, on the Somerset and Dorset border. Just before reaching Hemstridge from Milborne Port, at the cross-roads, there is a public-house called the Virginia Inn. There, it is said, according to Mr. Edward Hutton, in his "Highways and Byways in Somerset," "Sir Walter Raleigh smoked his first pipe of tobacco, and, being discovered by his servant, was drenched with a bucket of water."

At the fifteenth-century Manor-House at South Wraxall, Wiltshire, the "Raleigh Room" is shown, and visitors are told that according to local tradition it was in this room that Sir Walter smoked his first pipe, when visiting his friend, the owner of the mansion, Sir Henry Long.

Another tradition gives the old Pied Bull at Islington, long since demolished, as the scene of the momentous event. It is said in its earlier days to have been a country house of Sir Walter's, and according to legend it was in his dining-room in this house that he had his first pipe. Hone, in the first volume of the "Every Day Book" tells how he and some friends visited this Pied Bull, then in a very decayed condition, and smoked their pipes in the dining-room in memory of Sir Walter. From the recently published biography of William Hone by Mr. F.W. Hackwood, we learn that the jovial party consisted of William Hone, George Cruikshank, Joseph Goodyear, and David Sage, who jointly signed a humorous memorandum of their proceedings on the occasion, from which it appears that "each of us smoked a pipe, that is to say, each of us one or more pipes, or less than one pipe, and the undersigned George Cruikshank having smoked pipes innumerable or more or less," and that "several pots of porter, in aid of the said smoking," were consumed, followed by bowls of negus made from "port wine @ 3s. 6d. per bottle (duty knocked off lately)" and other ingredients. Speeches were made and toasts proposed, and altogether the four, who desired to "have the gratification of saying hereafter that we had smoked a pipe in the same room that the man who first introduced tobacco smoked in himself," seem to have thoroughly enjoyed themselves.

Wherever Raleigh is known to have lived or lodged we are sure to find the tradition flourishing that there he smoked his first pipe. The assertion has been made of his birthplace, Hayes Barton, although it is very doubtful if he ever visited the place after his parents left it, some years before their son had become acquainted with tobacco; and also with more plausibility of his home at Youghal, in the south of Ireland. Froude, in one of his "Short Studies," quotes a legend to the effect that Raleigh smoked on a rock below the Manor House of Greenaway, on the River Dart, which was the home of the first husband of Katherine Champernowne, afterwards Raleigh's wife; and Devonshire guide-books have adopted the story.

Perhaps the most likely scene of Raleigh's first experiments in the art of smoking was Durham House, which stood where the Adelphi Terrace and the streets between it and the Strand now stand. This was in the occupation of Sir Walter for twenty years (1583-1603), and he was probably resident there when Hariot returned from Virginia to make his report and instruct his employer in the management of a pipe. Walter Thornbury, in his "Haunted London," referring to the story of the servant throwing the ale over his smoking master, says: "There is a doubtful old legend about Raleigh's first pipe, the scene of which may be not unfairly laid at Durham House, where Raleigh lived." The ale story is mythical, but it is highly probable that Sir Walter's first pipes were smoked in Durham House. Dr. Brushfield quotes Hepworth Dixon, in "Her Majesty's Tower," as drawing "an imaginary and yet probable picture of him and his companions at a window of this very house, overlooking the 'silent highway':

"'It requires no effort of the fancy to picture these three men [Shakespeare, Bacon and Raleigh] as lounging in a window of Durham House, puffing the new Indian weed from silver bowls, discussing the highest themes in poetry and science, while gazing on the flower-beds and the river, the darting barges of dame and cavalier, and the distant pavilions of Paris garden and the Globe.'" This is a pure "effort of the fancy" so far as Bacon and Shakespeare are concerned. Shakespeare's absolute silence about tobacco forbids us to assume that he smoked; but of Raleigh the picture may be true enough. The house had, as Aubrey tells us, "a little turret that looked into and over the Thames, and had the prospect which is as pleasant perhaps as any in the world"; and it would be strange indeed if the owner of the noble house did not often smoke a contemplative pipe in the window of that pleasant turret.

The only mention made of tobacco by Raleigh himself occurs in a testamentary note made a little while before his execution in 1618. Referring to the tobacco remaining on his ship after his last voyage, he wrote: "Sir Lewis Stukely sold all the tobacco at Plimouth of which, for the most part of it, I gave him a fift part of it, as also a role for my Lord Admirall and a role for himself ... I desire that hee may give his account for the tobacco." As showing how closely Sir Walter's name was associated with it long after his death, Dr. Brushfield quotes the following entry from the diary of the great Earl of Cork: "Sept. 1, 1641. Sent by Travers to my infirme cozen Roger Vaghan, a pott of Sir Walter Raleighes tobackoe."

In the Wallace Collection at Hertford House is a pouch or case labelled as having belonged to and been used by Sir Walter Raleigh. This pouch contains several clay pipes. It was perhaps this same pouch or case which once upon a time figured in Ralph Thoresby's museum at Leeds, and is described by Thoresby himself in his "Ducatus Leodiensis," 1715. Curiously enough, a few years ago when excavations were being made around the foundations of Raleigh's house at Youghal a clay pipe-bowl was dug up which in size, shape, &c., was exactly like the pipes in the Wallace exhibit. Raleigh lived and no doubt smoked in the Youghal house, so it is quite possible that the bowl found belonged to one of the pipes actually smoked by him. In the garden of the Youghal house, by the way, they used to show the tree--perhaps still do so--under which Raleigh was sitting, smoking his pipe, when his servant drenched him. Thus the tradition, which, as we have seen, dates from 1708 only, has obtained two local habitations--Youghal and Durham House on the Adelphi site.

In November 1911 a curiously shaped pipe was put up for sale in Mr. J.C. Stevens's Auction Room, Covent Garden, which was described as that which Raleigh smoked "on the scaffold." The pipe in question was said to have been given by the doomed man to Bishop Andrewes, in whose family it remained for many years, and it was stated to have been in the family of the owner, who sent it for sale, for some 200 years. The pipe was of wood constructed in four pieces of strange shape, rudely carved with dogs' heads and faces of Red Indians. According to legend it had been presented to Raleigh by the Indians. The auctioneer, Mr. Stevens, remarked that unfortunately a parchment document about the pipe was lost some years ago, and declared, "If we could only produce the parchment the pipe would fetch L500." In the end, however, it was knocked down at seventy-five guineas.

The form and make of the first pipe is a matter I do not propose to go into here; but in connexion with the first pipe smoked in this country Aubrey's interesting statements must be given. Writing in the time of Charles II, he said that he had heard his grandfather say that at first one pipe was handed from man to man round about the table. "They had first silver pipes; the ordinary sort made use of a walnut shell and a straw"--surely a very unsatisfactory pipe. Tobacco in those earliest days, he says, was sold for its weight in silver. "I have heard some of our old yeomen neighbours say that when they went to Malmesbury or Chippenham Market, they culled out their biggest shillings to lay in the scales against the tobacco."

II
TOBACCO TRIUMPHANT: SMOKING FASHIONABLE AND UNIVERSAL

Tobacco engages
Both sexes, all ages,
The poor as well as the wealthy;
From the court to the cottage,
From childhood to dotage,
Both those that are sick and the healthy.
Wits' Recreations, 1640.

This chapter and the next deal with the history of smoking during the first fifty years after its introduction as a social habit--roughly to 1630. The use of tobacco spread with extraordinary rapidity among all classes of society. During the latter part of Queen Elizabeth's reign and through the early decades of the seventeenth century tobacco-pipes were in full blast. Tobacco was triumphant.

Perhaps the most noteworthy thing about smoking at this period, from the social point of view, was its fashionableness. One of the marked characteristics of the gallant--the beau or dandy or "swell" of the time--was his devotion to tobacco. Earle says that a gallant was one that was born and shaped for his clothes--but clothes were only a part of his equipment. Bishop Hall, satirizing the young man of fashion in 1597, describes the delicacies with which he was accustomed to indulge his appetite, and adds that, having eaten, he "Quaffs a whole tunnel of tobacco smoke"; and old Robert Burton, in satirically enumerating the accomplishments of "a complete, a well-qualified gentleman," names to "take tobacco with a grace," with hawking, riding, hunting, card-playing, dicing and the like. The qualifications for a gallant were described by another writer in 1603 as "to make good faces, to take Tobacco well, to spit well, to laugh like a waiting gentlewoman, to lie well, to blush for nothing, to looke big upon little fellowes, to scoffe with a grace ... and, for a neede, to ride prettie and well."

A curious feature of tobacco-manners among fashionable smokers of the period was the practice of passing a pipe from one to another, after the fashion of the "loving cup." There is a scene in "Greene's Tu Quoque," 1614, laid in a fashionable ordinary, where the London gallants meet as usual, and one says to a companion who is smoking: "Please you to impart your smoke?" "Very willingly, sir," says the smoker. Number two takes a whiff or two and courteously says: "In good faith, a pipe of excellent vapour!" The owner of the pipe then explains that it is "the best the house yields," whereupon the other immediately depreciates it, saying affectedly: "Had you it in the house? I thought it had been your own: 'tis not so good now as I took it for!" Another writer of this time speaks of one pipe of tobacco sufficing "three or four men at once."

The rich young gallant carried about with him his tobacco apparatus (often of gold or silver) in the form of tobacco-box, tobacco-tongs--wherewith to lift a live coal to light his pipe, ladle "for the cold snuffe into the nosthrill," and priming-iron. Sometimes the tobacco-box was of ivory; and occasionally a gallant would have looking-glass set in his box, so that when he took it out to obtain tobacco, he could at the same time have a view of his own delectable person. When our gallant went to dine at the ordinary, according to the custom of the time, he brought out these possessions, and smoked while the dinner was being served. Before dinner, after taking a few turns up and down Paul's Walk in the old cathedral, he might look into the booksellers' shops, and, pipe in mouth, inquire for the most recent attack upon the "divine weed"--the contemporary tobacco literature was abundant--or drop into an apothecary's, which was usually a tobacco-shop also, and there meet his fellow-smokers.

In the afternoon the gallant might attend what Dekker calls a "Tobacco-ordinary," by which may possibly have been meant a smoking-club, or, more probably, the gathering after dinner at one of the many ordinaries in the neighbourhood of St. Paul's Cathedral of "tobacconists," as smokers were then called, to discuss the merits of their respective pipes, and of the various kinds of tobacco--"whether your Cane or your Pudding be sweetest."

Of course he often bragged, like Julio in Day's "Law Trickes": "Tobacco? the best in Europe, 't cost me ten Crownes an ounce, by this vapour."

An amusing example of the bragging "tobacconist" is pictured for us in Ben Jonson's "Bobadil." Bobadil may perhaps be somewhat of an exaggerated carica-ture, but it is probable that the dramatist in drawing him simply exaggerated the characteristic traits of many smokers of the day. This hero, drawing tobacco from his pocket, declares that it is all that is left of seven pounds which he had bought only "yesterday was seven-night." A consumption of seven pounds of tobacco in eight days is a pretty "tall order"! Then he goes on to brag of its quality--your right Trinidado--and to assert that he had been in the Indies, where the herb grows, and where he himself and a dozen other gentlemen had for the space of one-and-twenty weeks known no other nutriment than the fume of tobacco. This again was toler-ably "steep" even for this Falstaff-like braggart. He continues with more bombast in praise of the medicinal virtues of the herb--virtues which were then very firmly and widely believed in--and is replied to by Cob, the anti-tobacconist, who, with equal exaggeration on the other side, denounces tobacco, and declares that four people had died in one house from the use of it in the preceding week, and that one had "voided a bushel of soot"!

The properly accomplished gallant not only professed to be curiously learned in pipes and tobacco, but his knowledge of prices and their fluctuations, of the apothecaries' and other shops where the herb was sold, and of the latest and most fashionable ways of inhaling and exhaling the smoke, was, like Mr. Weller's knowl-edge of London, "extensive and peculiar." It was knowledge of this kind that gained for a gallant reputation and respect by no means to be acquired by mere scholarship and learning.

The satirical Dekker might class "tobacconists" with "feather-makers, cobweb-lawne-weavers, perfumers, young country gentlemen and fools," but he bears in-valuable witness to the devotion of the fashionable men of the day to the "costlye and gentleman-like Smoak."

It was customary for a man to carry a case of pipes about with him. In a play of 1609 ("Everie Woman in her Humour") there is an inventory of the contents of a gentleman's pocket, with a value given for each item, which displays certainly a curious assortment of articles. First comes a brush and comb worth fivepence, and next a looking-glass worth three halfpence. With these aids to vanity are a case of tobacco-pipes valued at fourpence, half an ounce of tobacco valued at sixpence, and three pence in coin, or, as it is quaintly worded, "in money and golde." Satirists of course made fun of the smoker's pocketful of apparatus. A pamphleteer of 1609 says: "I behelde pipes in his pocket; now he draweth forth his tinder-box and his touchwood, and falleth to his tacklings; sure his throat is on fire, the smoke flyeth so fast from his mouth."

It may be noted, by the way, that the gallant had no hesitation about smoking in the presence of ladies. Gostanzo, in Chapman's "All Fools," 1605, says:

And for discourse in my fair mistress's presence
I did not, as you barren gallants do,
Fill my discourses up drinking tobacco.

And in Ben Jonson's "Every Man out of his Humour," 1600, Fastidious Brisk, "a neat, spruce, affecting courtier," smokes while he talks to his mistress. A feather-headed gallant, when in the presence of ladies, often found himself, like others of his tribe of later date, gravelled for lack of matter for conversation, and the puffing of tobacco-smoke helped to occupy the pauses.

When our gallant went to the theatre he loved to occupy one of the stools at the side of the stage. There he could sit and smoke and embarrass the actors with his audible criticisms of play and players.

It chaunc'd me gazing at the Theater,
To spie a Lock-Tabacco Chevalier
Clowding the loathing ayr with foggie fume
Of Dock Tobacco friendly foe to rhume --

says a versifier of 1599, who did not like smoking in the theatre and so abused the quality of the tobacco smoked--though admitting its medicinal virtue. Dekker suggests, probably with truth, that one reason why the young gallant liked to push his way to a stool on the stage, notwithstanding "the mewes and hisses of the op-posed rascality"--the "mewes" must have been the squeals or whistles produced by the instrument which was later known as a cat-call--was the opportunity such a prominent position afforded for the display of "the best and most essential parts of a gallant--good cloathes, a proportionable legge, white hand, the Persian lock, and a tolerable beard." Apparently, too, serving-boys were within call, and thus lights could easily be obtained, which were handed to one another by the smokers on the points of their swords.

Ben Jonson has given us an amusing picture of the behaviour of gallants on the Elizabethan stage, in his "Cynthia's Revels." In this scene a child thus mim-ics the obtrusive beau: "Now, sir, suppose I am one of your genteel auditors, that am come in (having paid my money at the door, with much ado), and here I take my place, and sit downe. I have my three sorts of tobacco in my pocket, my light by me, and thus I begin. 'By this light, I wonder that any man is so mad, to come to see these rascally tits play here--they do act like so many wrens--not the fifth part of a good face amongst them all--and then their musick is abominable--able to stretch a man's ears worse than ten--pillories, and their ditties--most lamentable things, like the pitiful fellows that make them--poets. By this vapour--an't were not for tobacco--I think--the very smell of them would poison me, I should not dare to come in at their gates. A man were better visit fifteen jails--or a dozen or two hospitals--than once adventure to come near them.'" And the young rascal, who at each pause marked by a dash had puffed his pipe, no doubt blowing an extra large "cloud" when he swore "by this vapour," turns to his companions and says: "How is't? Well?" and they pronounce his mimicry "Excellent!"

Smoking was not confined to the auditors on the stage, who paid sixpence each for a stool. There was the "lords' room" over the stage, which seems to have cor-responded with the modern stage boxes, the price of admission to which appears to have been a shilling, where the pipe was also in full blast. Dekker tells how a gallant at a new play would take a place in the "twelve penny room, next the stage, because the lords and you may seem to be hail fellow, well met"; and Jonson, in "Every Man out of his Humour," 1600, speaks of one who pretended familiarity with courtiers, that he talked of them as if he had "taken tobacco with them over the stage, in the lords' room."

Among the general audience of the theatre smoking seems to have been usual also. The anti-tobacconists among those present, few of whom were men, must have suffered by the practice. In that admirable burlesque comedy by Beaumont and Fletcher, "The Knight of the Burning Pestle," 1613, the citizen's wife, addressing herself either to the gallants on the stage, or to her fellow-spectators sitting around her, exclaims: "Fy! This stinking tobacco kills men! Would there were none in England! Now I pray, gentlemen, what good does this stinking tobacco do you? Nothing, I warrant you; make chimneys a' your faces!" But many women viewed tobacco differently, as we shall see in the chapter on "Smoking by Women." Moreover, this good woman herself, in the epilogue to the burlesque, invites the gentlemen whom she has before abused for smoking, to come to her house where she will entertain them with "a pottle of wine, and a pipe of tobacco."

Hentzner, the German traveller, who visited London in 1598, speaks of smoking being customary among the audience at plays, who were also supplied with "fruits, such as apples, pears and nuts, according to the season, carried about to be sold, as well as ale and wine." He was struck with the universal prevalence of the tobacco-habit. Not only at plays, but "everywhere else," he says, the "English are constantly smoking tobacco," and then he proceeds to describe how they did it: "They have pipes on purpose made of clay, into the further end of which they put the herb, so dry that it may be rubbed into powder; and putting fire to it, they draw the smoak into their mouths, which they puff out again through their nostrils, like funnels, along with it plenty of phlegm and defluxions from the head." This suggests that the unpleasant and quite unnecessary habit of spitting was common with these early smokers, a suggestion which is amply supported by other contemporary evidence.

Tobacco was smoked by all classes and in almost all places. It was smoked freely in the streets. In some verses prefixed to an edition of Skelton's "Elinour Rumming" which appeared in 1624, the ghost of Skelton, who was poet-laureate to King Henry VIII, was made to say that he constantly saw smoking:

As I walked between
Westminster Hall
And the Church of Saint Paul,

And so thorow the citie,
Where I saw and did pitty
My country men's cases,
With fiery-smoke faces,
Sucking and drinking
A filthie weede stinking.

Tobacco-selling was sometimes curiously combined with other trades. A Fleet Street tobacconist of this time was also a dealer in worsted stockings. A mercer of Mansfield who died at the beginning of 1624, and who apparently carried on business also at Southwell, had a considerable stock of tobacco. In the Inventory of all his "cattalles and goods" which is dated 24 January 1624, there is included "It. in Tobacco 19.li 0. 0." Nineteen pounds' worth of tobacco, considering the then value of money, was no small stock for a mercer-tobacconist to carry.

But the apothecaries were the most usual salesmen, and their shops and the ordinaries were the customary day meeting-places for the more fashionable smokers. The taverns and inns, however, were also filled with smoke, and taverns were frequented by men of all social grades. Dekker speaks of the gallant leaving the tavern at night when "the spirit of wine and tobacco walkes" in his train. On the occasion of the accession of James I, 1603, when London was given up to rejoicing and revelry, we are told that "tobacconists [i.e. smokers] filled up whole Tavernes."

King James himself is an unwilling witness to the popularity of tobacco. He tells us that a man could not heartily welcome his friend without at once proposing a smoke. It had become, he says, a point of good-fellowship, and he that would refuse to take a pipe among his fellows was accounted "peevish and no good company." "Yea," he continues, with rising indignation, "the mistress cannot in a more mannerly kind entertain her servant than by giving him out of her fair hand a pipe of tobacco."

Smoking was soon as common in the country as in London. On Wednesday, April 16, 1621, in the course of a debate in the House of Commons, Sir William Stroud, who seems to have been a worthy disciple of that tobacco-hater, King James I, moved that he "would have tobacco banished wholly out of the kingdom, and that it may not be brought in from any part, nor used amongst us"; and Sir Grey

Palmes said "that if tobacco be not banished, it will overthrow 100,000 men in England, for now it is so common that he hath seen ploughmen take it as they are at plough." Perhaps this terrible picture of a ploughman smoking as he followed his lonely furrow did not impress the House so much as Sir Grey evidently thought it would; at all events, tobacco was not banished.

Peers and squires and parsons and peasants alike smoked. The parson of Thornton, in Buckinghamshire, was so devoted to tobacco that when his supply of the weed ran short, he is said to have cut up the bell-ropes and smoked them! This is dated about 1630. In the well-known description of the famous country squire, Mr. Hastings, who was remarkable for keeping up old customs in the early years of the seventeenth century, we read of how his hall tables were littered with hawks' hoods, bells, old hats with their crowns thrust in, full of pheasants' eggs; tables, dice, cards, and store of tobacco-pipes.

Sir Francis Vere, in the account of his services by sea and land which he wrote about 1606, mentions that on an expedition to the Azores in 1597, the Earl of Essex, waiting for news of the enemy at St. Michael, "called for tobacco ... and so on horseback, with those Noblemen and Gentlemen on foot beside him, took tobacco, whilst I was telling his Lordship of the men I had sent forth, and orders I had given." Presently came the sound of guns, which "made his Lordship cast his pipe from him, and listen to the shooting."

Another famous nobleman, Lord Herbert of Cherbury--

All-virtuous Herbert! on whose every part
Truth might spend all her voice, fame all her art!--

was a smoker, as we know from a very curious passage in his well-known autobiography. He appears to have smoked not so much for pleasure as for supposed reasons of health. "It is well known," he wrote, "to those that wait in my chamber, that the shirts, waistcoats, and other garments I wear next my body, are sweet, beyond what either can easily be believed, or hath been observed in any else, which sweetness also was found to be in my breath above others, before I used to take tobacco, which towards my latter time I was forced to take against certain rheums and catarrhs that trouble me, which yet did not taint my breath for any long time."

The autobiography was written about 1645, so as Lord Herbert did not smoke till towards the latter part of his life--he died in 1648--he clearly was not one of those who took to tobacco in the first enthusiasm for the new indulgence.

When Robert, Earl of Essex, and Henry, Earl of Southampton, were tried for high treason in Westminster Hall on February 19, 1600-1, the members of the House of Lords, who with the Judges formed the Court, if we may believe the French Ambassador of the time, behaved in a remarkable and unseemly manner. In a letter to Monsieur de Rohan, the Ambassador declared that while the Earls and the Counsel were pleading, their lordships guzzled and smoked; and that when they gave their votes condemning the two Earls, they were stupid with eating and "yvres de tabac"--drunk with smoking. This was probably quite untrue as a representation of what actually took place; but it would hardly have been written had smoking not been a common practice among noble lords.

Queen Elizabeth's Secretary of State, Sir Robert Cecil, would appear to have been a smoker. In a letter addressed to him, John Watts, an alderman of London, wrote: "According to your request, I have sent the greatest part of my store of tobaca by the bearer, wishing that the same may be to your good liking. But this tobaca I have had this six months, which was such as my son brought home, but since that time I have had none. At this period there is none that is good to be had for money. Wishing you to make store thereof, for I do not know where to have the like, I have sent you of two sorts. Mincing Lane, 12 Dec. 1600."

A curious scene took place at Oxford in 1605 when King James visited the University. Two subjects were debated by learned dons before his Majesty, and one of them, at his own suggestion, was, "Whether the frequent use of tobacco is good for healthy men?" Among those who spoke were Doctors Ailworth, Gwyn, Gifford and Cheynell. The discussion, needless to say, being conducted in the presence of the author of the "Counterblaste to Tobacco," was not favourable to the herb. The King summed up in a speech which hopelessly begged the question while it contained plenty of strong denunciation. After his Majesty had spoken, one learned doctor, Cheynell, who is described by the recorder, Isaac Wake, the Public Orator of the University, as second to none of the doctors, had the courage to rise and, with a pipe held forth in his hand, to speak both wittily and eloquently in favour of tobacco from the medicinal point of view, praising it to the skies, says Wake, as of virtue beyond all other remedial agents. His wit pleased both the King and the whole assembly, whom it moved to laughter; but when he had finished, his Majesty made a lengthy rejoinder in which he said some curious things. He objected to the medicinal use of tobacco, and quite agreed with previous speakers that such a use must have arisen among Barbarians and Indians, who he went on to say had as much knowledge of medicine as they had of civilized customs. If, he argued, there were men whose bodies were benefited by tobacco-smoke, this did not so much redound to the credit of tobacco, as it did reflect upon the depraved condition of such men, that their bodies should have sunk to the level of those of Barbarians so as to be affected by remedies such as were effective on the bodies of Barbarians and Indians! His Majesty kindly suggested that doctors who believed in tobacco as a remedial agent should take themselves and their medicine of pollution off to join the Indians.

III
TOBACCO TRIUMPHANT (continued) --SELLERS OF TOBACCO AND PROFESSORS OF SMOKING--ABUSE AND PRAISE OF TOBACCO

> This is my friend Abel, an honest fellow;
> He lets me have good tobacco.
> BEN JONSON, The Alchemist.

The druggists and other tradesmen who sold tobacco in Elizabethan and Jacobean days had every provision for the convenience of their numerous customers. Some so-called druggists, it may be shrewdly suspected, did much more business in tobacco than they did in drugs. Dekker tells us of an apothecary and his wife who had no customers resorting to their shop "for any phisicall stuffe," but whose shop had many frequenters in the shape of gentlemen who "came to take their pipes of the divine smoake." That tobacco was often the most profitable part of a druggist's stock is also clear from the last sentence in Bishop Earle's character of "A Tobacco-Seller," one of the shortest in that remarkable collection of "Characters" which the Bishop issued in 1628 under the title of "Micro-Cosmographie."

"A Tobacco-Seller," says Earle, "is the onely man that findes good in it which others brag of, but do not; for it is meate, drinke, and clothes to him. No man opens his ware with greater seriousnesse, or challenges your judgement more in the approbation. His shop is the Randevous of spitting, where men dialogue with their noses, and their communication is smoake. It is the place onely where Spaine is commended, and prefer'd before England itselfe. He should be well experienc'd in the world: for he ha's daily tryall of mens nostrils, and none is better acquainted with humors. Hee is the piecing commonly of some other trade which is bawde to his Tobacco, and that to his wife, which is the flame that follows this smoke."

This brief "Character" is hardly so pointed or so effective as some of the others in the "Micro-Cosmographie," but it would seem that the Bishop was not very friendly to tobacco. In the character of "A Drunkard" he says: "Tobacco serves to aire him after a washing [i.e. a drinking-bout], and is his onely breath, and breathing while." In another, a tavern "is the common consumption of the Afternoone, and the murderer, or maker away of a rainy day. It is the Torrid Zone that scorches the face, and Tobacco the gunpowder that blows it up."

The druggist-tobacconists were well stocked with abundance of pipes--those known as Winchester pipes were highly popular--with maple blocks for cutting or shredding the tobacco upon, juniper wood charcoal fires, and silver tongs with which the hot charcoal could be lifted to light the customer's pipe. The maple block was in constant use in those days, when the many present forms of prepared tobacco and varied mixtures were unknown. In Middleton and Dekker's "Roaring Girl," 1611, the "mincing and shredding of tobacco" is mentioned; and in the same play, by the way, we are told that "a pipe of rich smoak" was sold for sixpence.

The tobacco-tongs were more properly called ember-or brand-tongs. They sometimes had a tobacco-stopper riveted in near the axis of the tongs, and thus could be easily distinguished from other kinds of tongs. An example in the Guildhall Museum, made of brass, and probably of late seventeenth-century date, has the end of one of the handles formed into a stopper. In the same collection there are several pairs of ember-tongs with handles or jaws decorated. In one or two a handle terminates in a hook, by which they could be hung up when not required for use. In that delightful book of pictures and gossip concerning old household and farming gear, and old-fashioned domestic plenishings of many kinds, called "Old West Surrey," Miss Jekyll figures two pairs of old ember-or brand-tongs. One of these quite deserves the praise which she bestows upon it. "Its lines," says Miss Jekyll, "fill one with the satisfaction caused by a thing that is exactly right, and with admiration for the art and skill of a true artist." These homely tongs are fashioned with a fine eye for symmetry, and, indeed, for beauty of design and perfect fitness for the intended purpose. The ends which were to pick up the coal are shaped like two little hands, while "the edges have slight mouldings and even a low bead enrichment. The circular flat on the side away from the projecting stopper has two tiny engraved pictures; on one side of the joint a bottle and tall wine-glass, on the other a pair of long clay pipes crossed, and a bowl of tobacco shown in section." This beautiful little implement bears the engraved name of its Surrey maker, and the date 1795.

Country-folk nowadays often light their pipes in the old way, by picking up a live coal, or, in Ireland, a fragment of glowing peat, from the kitchen fire, with the ordinary tongs, and applying it to the pipe-bowl; but the old ember-tongs are seldom seen. They may still be found in some farmhouses and country cottages, which have not been raided by the agents of dealers in antique furniture and implements, but examples are rare. This is a digression, however, which has carried us far away from the early years of the seventeenth century.

It is pretty clear that not a few of the druggists who sold tobacco were great rascals. Ben Jonson has let us into some of their secrets of adulteration--the treatment of the leaf with oil and the lees of sack, the increase of its weight by other artificial additions to its moisture, washing it in muscadel and grains, keeping it in greased leather and oiled rags buried in gravel under ground, and by like devices. Other writers speak of black spice, galanga, aqua vitae, Spanish wine, aniseeds and other things as being used for purposes of adulteration.

Trickery of another kind is revealed in a scene in Chapman's play "A Humorous Day's Mirth," 1599. A customer at an ordinary says: "Hark you, my host, have you a pipe of good tobacco?" "The best in the town," says mine host, after the manner of his class. "Boy, dry a leaf." Quietly the boy tells him, "There's none in the house, sir," to which the worthy host replies sotto voce , "Dry a dock leaf." But the diner's potations must have been powerful if they had left him unable to distinguish between the taste of tobacco and that of dried dock-leaf.

Sometimes coltsfoot was mixed with tobacco. Ursula, the pig-woman and refreshment-booth keeper in Bartholomew Fair, in Ben Jonson's play of that name, says to her assistant: "Threepence a pipe-full I will have made, of all my whole half-pound of tobacco and a quarter of a pound of coltsfoot mixt with it too to eke it out."

The fumes of dried coltsfoot leaves were used as a remedy in cases of difficulty of breathing, both in ancient Roman times and in Tudor England. Lyte, in his translation, 1578, of Dodoens' "Historie of Plants," says of coltsfoot: "The parfume of the dryed leaves layde upon quicke coles, taken into the mouth through the pipe of a funnell, or tunnell, helpeth suche as are troubled with the shortnesse of winde, and fetche their breath thicke or often, and do [sic] breake without daunger the impostems of the breast." The leaves of coltsfoot and of other plants have often been used as a substitute for tobacco in modern days. A correspondent of Notes and Queries, in 1897, said that when he was a boy he knew an old Calvinist minister, who used to smoke a dried mixture of the leaves of horehound, yarrow and "foal's foot" intermingled with a small quantity of tobacco. He said it was a very good substitute for the genuine article. Similar mixtures, or the leaves of coltsfoot alone, have often been smoked in bygone days by folk who could not afford to smoke tobacco only.

The number of shops where tobacco was sold in the early days of its triumph seems to have been extraordinary. Barnaby Rich, one of the most prolific parents of pamphlets in an age of prolific writers, wrote a satire on "The Honestie of this Age," which was printed in 1614. In this production Rich declares that every fellow who came into an ale-house and called for his pot, must have his pipe also, for tobacco was then a commodity as much sold in every tavern, inn and ale-house as wine, ale, or beer. He goes on to say that apothecaries' shops, grocers' shops, and chandlers' shops were (almost) never without company who from morning to night were still taking tobacco; and what a number there are besides, he adds, "that doe keepe houses, set open shoppes, that have no other trade to live by but by the selling of tobacco." Rich says he had been told that a list had been recently made of all the houses that traded in tobacco in and near about London, and that if a man might believe what was confidently reported, there were found to be upwards of 7000 houses that lived by that trade; but he could not say whether the apothecaries', grocers' and chandlers' shops, where tobacco was also sold, were included in that number. He proceeds to calculate what the annual expenditure on smoke must be. The number of 7000 seems very large and is perhaps exaggerated. Round numbers are apt to be over rather than under the mark.

Another proof of the extraordinary popularity of the new habit is to be found in the fact that by the seventeenth year of the reign of James I--the arch-enemy of tobacco--that is, by 1620, the Society of Tobacco-pipe-makers had become so very numerous and considerable a body that they were incorporated by royal charter, and bore on their shield a tobacco plant in full blossom. The Society's motto was happily chosen--"Let brotherly love continue."

A further witness to the prevalence of smoking and to the enormous number of tobacco-sellers' shops is Camden, the antiquary. In his "Annales," 1625, he remarks with curious detail that since its introduction--"that Indian plant called Tobacco, or Nicotiana, is growne so frequent in use and of such price, that many, nay, the most part, with an insatiable desire doe take of it, drawing into their mouth the smoke thereof, which is of a strong scent, through a pipe made of earth, and venting of it againe through their nose; some for wantownesse, or rather fashion sake, and other for health sake, insomuch that Tobacco shops are set up in greater number than either Alehouses or Tavernes."

One result of the herb's popularity was found in frequent attempts by trades-men of various kinds to sell it without being duly licensed to do so. Mr. W.G. Bell, in his valuable book on "Fleet Street in Seven Centuries," mentions the arrest of a Fleet Street grocer by the Star Chamber for unlicensed trading in tobacco. He also quotes from the St. Dunstan's Wardmote Register of 1630 several cases of complaint against unlicensed traders and others. Four men were presented "for selling ale and tobacco unlicensed, and for annoying the Judges of Serjeants Inn whose chambers are near adjoyning." Two other men, one of them hailing from the notorious Ram Alley, were presented "for annoying the Judges at Serjeants Inn with the stench and smell of their tobacco," which looks as if the Judges were of King James's mind about smoking. The same Register of 1630 records the presentment of two men of the same family name--Thomas Bouringe and Philip Bouringe--"for keeping open their shops and selling tobacco at unlawful hours, and having disorderly people in their house to the great disturbance of all the inhabitants and neighbours near adjoining." The Ram Alley, Fleet Street, mentioned above, was notorious in sundry ways. Mr. Bell mentions that in 1618 the wardmote laid complaint against Timothy Louse and John Barker, of Ram Alley, "for keeping their tobacco-shoppes open all night and fyers in the same without any chimney and suffering hot waters [spirits] and selling also without licence, to the great disquietness and annoyance of that neighbourhood." There were sad goings on of many kinds in Ram Alley.

It is uncertain when licences were first issued for the sale of tobacco. Probably they were issued in London some time before it was considered necessary to license dealers in other parts of the country. Among the Municipal Records of Exeter is the following note: "358. Whitehall, 31 August 1633. The Lords of the Council to the Chamber. 'Whereas his Matie to prevent the excesse of the use of Tobacco, and to set an order to those that regrate and sell or utter it by retayle, who observe noe reasonable rates or prizes [prices], nor take care that it be wholsome for men's bodyes that shall use it,' has caused letters to be sent to the chief Officers of Citties and towns requiring them to certify 'in what places it might be fitt to suffer ye retayleing of Tobacco and how many be licenced in each of those places to use trade'; and the City of Exeter having made a return the Lords sent a list of those which are to be licensed, and order that no others be permitted to sell."

In the neighbouring county of Somerset the Justices of the Peace sent presentments to the Council in 1632 of persons within the Hundred of Milverton and Kingsbury West thought fit to sell tobacco by retail; and for Wiveliscombe, Mr. Hancock says in his book on that old town, a mercer and a hosier were selected.

It would seem, from one example I have noted, as if in some places smoking were not allowed in public-houses. In the account-book of St. Stephen's Church and Parish, Norwich, the income for the year 1628-29 included on one occasion 20s. received by way of fine from one Edmond Nockals for selling a pot of beer "wanting in measure, contrary to the law," and another sovereign from William Howlyns for a like offence. This is right and intelligible enough; but on another occasion in the same year each of these men, who presumably were ale-house keepers, had to pay 30s.--a substantial sum considering the then value of money--for the same offence and "for suffering parishioners to smoke in his house." I have been unable to obtain any information as to why a publican should have been fined an additional 10s. for the heinous offence of allowing a brother parishioner to smoke in his house.

Penalties for "offences" of this fanciful kind were not common in England; but in Puritan New England they were abundant. In the early days of the American Colonies the use of the "creature called Tobacko" was by no means encouraged. In Connecticut a man was permitted by the law to smoke once if he went on a journey of ten miles, but not more than once a day and by no means in another man's house. It could hardly have been difficult to evade so absurd a regulation as this.

It has been already stated that the Elizabethan gallant was acquainted with the most fashionable methods of inhaling and exhaling the smoke of tobacco. A singular feature of the enthusiasm for tobacco in the early years of the seventeenth century was the existence of professors of the art of smoking.

Some of the apothecaries whose shops were in most repute for the quality of the tobacco kept, took pupils and taught them the "slights," as tricks with the pipe were called. These included exhaling the smoke in little globes, rings and so forth. The invaluable Ben Jonson, in the preliminary account of the characters in his "Every Man out of his Humour," 1600, describes one Sogliardo as "an essential clown ... yet so enamoured of the name of a gentleman that he will have it though he buys it. He comes up every term to learn to take tobacco and see new motions." Sogliardo was accustomed to hire a private room to practise in. The fashionable way was to expel the smoke through the nose. In a play by Field of 1618, a foolish nobleman is asked by some boon companions in a tavern: "Will your lordship take any tobacco?" when another sneers, "'Sheart! he cannot put it through his nose!" His lordship was apparently not well versed in the "slights."

Taking tobacco was clearly an accomplishment to be studied seriously. Shift, a professor of the art in Jonson's play, puts up a bill in St. Paul's--the recognized centre for advertisements and commercial business of every kind--in which he offers to teach any young gentleman newly come into his inheritance, who wishes to be as exactly qualified as the best of the ordinary-hunting gallants are--"to entertain the most gentlemanlike use of tobacco; as first, to give it the most exquisite perfume; then to know all the delicate sweet forms for the assumption of it; as also the rare corollary and practice of the Cuban ebolition, euripus and whiff, which he shall receive, or take in here at London, and evaporate at Uxbridge, or farther, if it please him."

Taking the whiff, it has been suggested, may have been either a swallowing of the smoke, or a retaining it in the throat for a given space of time; but what may be meant by the "Cuban ebolition" or the "euripus" is perhaps best left to the imagination. "Ebolition" is simply a variant of "ebullition," and "ebullition," as applied with burlesque intent to rapid smoking--the vapour bubbling rapidly from the pipe-bowl--is intelligible enough, but why Cuban? "Euripus" was the name, in ancient geography, of the channel between Euboea (Negropont) and the mainland--a passage which was celebrated for the violence and uncertainty of its currents--and hence the name was occasionally applied by our older writers to any strait or sea-channel having like characteristics. The use of the word in connexion with tobacco may, like that of "ebolition," have some reference to furious smoking, but the meaning is not clear.

If one contemporary writer may be believed, some of these early smokers acquired the art of emitting the smoke through their ears, but a healthy scepticism is permissible here.

The accomplished Shift promises a would-be pupil in the art of taking tobacco that if he pleases to be a practitioner, he shall learn in a fortnight to "take it plausibly in any ordinary, theatre, or the Tiltyard, if need be, in the most popular assembly that is." The Tiltyard adjoined Whitehall Palace and was the frequent scene of sports in which Queen Elizabeth took the greatest delight. Here took place, not only tilting properly so called, but rope-walking performances, bear- and bull-baiting, dancing and other diversions which her Majesty held in high favour. Consequently the Tiltyard was constantly the scene of courtly gatherings; and if smoking were permitted on such occasions--as Shift's boasting promises would appear to indicate--then it may be reasonably inferred that Queen Elizabeth did not entertain the objections to the new practice that her successor, King James, set forth with such vehemence in his famous "Counterblaste to Tobacco." There is, however, no positive evidence one way or the other, to show what the attitude of the Virgin Queen towards tobacco really was. A tradition as to her smoking herself on one occasion is referred to in a subsequent chapter--that on "Smoking by Women."

Although tobacco was in such general use it yet had plenty of enemies. It was extravagantly abused and extravagantly praised. Robert Burton, of "Anatomy of Melancholy" fame, like many other writers of his time, was prepared to admit the medicinal value of the herb, though he detested the general habit of smoking. Tobacco was supposed in those days to be "good for" a surprising variety of ailments and diseases; but to explore that little section of popular medicine would be foreign to my purpose. Burton believed in tobacco as medicine; but with regard to habitual smoking he was a worthy follower of King James, the strength of whose language he sought to emulate and exceed when he denounced the common taking of tobacco "by most men, which take it as tinkers do ale"--as "a plague, a mischief, a violent purger of goods, lands, health, hellish, devilish, and damned tobacco, the ruin and overthrow of body and soul." No anti-tobacconist could wish for a more whole-hearted denunciation than that.

Thomas Dekker, to whose pictures of London social life at the opening of the seventeenth century we are so much indebted for information both with regard to smoking and in respect of many other matters of interest, was himself an enemy of tobacco. He politely refers to "that great Tobacconist, the Prince of Smoake and Darkness, Don Pluto"; and in another place addresses tobacco as "thou beggarly Monarche of Indians, and setter up of rotten-lungd chimney-sweepers," and proceeds in a like strain of abuse.

One of the most curious of the early publications on tobacco, in which an attempt is made to hold the balance fairly between the legitimate use and the "licentious" abuse of the herb, is Tobias Venner's tract with the long-winded title: "A Brief and Accurate Treatise concerning The taking of the Fume of Tobacco, Which very many, in these dayes doe too licenciously use. In which the immoderate, irregular, and unseasonable use thereof is reprehended, and the true nature and best manner of using it, perspicuously demonstrated." Venner described himself as a doctor of physic in Bath, and his tract was published in London in 1637. Venner says that tobacco is of "ineffable force" for the rapid healing of wounds, cuts, sores and so on, by external application, but thinks little of its use for any other purpose. Like others of his school, he attacks the "licentious Tobacconists [smokers] who spend and consume, not only their time, but also their health, wealth, and witts in taking of this loathsome and unsavorie fume." He admits the popularity of the herb, but expresses his own personal objection to the "detestable savour or smack that it leaveth behind upon the taking of it"; from which one is inclined to surmise that the doctor's first pipe was not an entire success. With an evident desire to be fair, Venner, notwithstanding his dislike of the "savour," refuses to condemn tobacco utterly, because of what he considers its valuable medicinal qualities, and he goes so far as to give "10 precepts in the use of" tobacco. The sixth is "that you drink not between the taking of the fumes, as our idle and smoakie Tobacconists are wont"--there must be no alliance, in short, between the pipe and the cheerful glass. The tenth and last precept is "that you goe not abroad into the aire presently [immediately] upon the taking of the fume, but rather refrain therefrom the space of halfe an houre, or more, especially if the season be cold, or moist." The suggestion that the smoker, when he has finished his pipe, shall wait for half an hour or so before he ventures into the outer air is very quaint.

Venner goes on to give a terrible catalogue of the ills that will befall the smoker who uses tobacco "contrary to the order and way I have set down." It is a dreadful list which may possibly have frightened a few nervous smokers; but probably it had no greater effect than the terrible curse in the "Jackdaw of Rheims."

Another tract which may be classed with Venner's "Treatise" was the "Nepenthes or the Vertues of Tobacco," by Dr. William Barclay, which was published at Edinburgh in 1614. This is sometimes referred to and quoted, as by Fairholt, as if it were a whole-hearted defence of tobacco-taking. But Barclay enlarges mainly on the medicinal virtues of the herb. "If Tabacco," he says, "were used physically and with discretion there were no medicament in the worlde comparable to it"; and again: "In Tabacco there is nothing which is not medicine, the root, the stalke, the leaves, the seeds, the smoake, the ashes." The doctor gives sundry directions for administering tobacco--"to be used in infusion, in decoction, in substance, in smoke, in salt." But Barclay clearly does not sympathize with its indiscriminate use for pleasure. "As concerning the smoke," he says, "it may be taken more frequently, and for the said effects, but always fasting, and with emptie stomack, not as the English abusers do, which make a smoke-boxe of their skull, more fit to be carried under his arme that selleth at Paris dunoir a noircir to blacke mens shooes then to carie the braine of him that can not walke, can not ryde except the Tabacco Pype be in his mouth." He goes on to say that he was once in company with an English merchant in Normandy--"betweene Rowen and New-haven"--who was a merry fellow, but was constantly wanting a coal to kindle his tobacco. "The Frenchman wondered and I laughed at his intemperancie."

It is a little curious, considering the devotion of latter-day men of letters to tobacco, that in their early days so many of the men who wrote on the subject attacked the social use of tobacco with violence and virulence. Perhaps, courtier-like, they followed the lead of the British Solomon, King James I. Their titles are characteristic of their style. A writer named Deacon published in 1616 a quarto entitled "Tobacco tortured in the filthy Fumes of Tobacco refined"; but Joshua Sylvester had easily surpassed this when he wrote his "Tobacco Battered and the Pipes Shattered about their Eares, that idely Idolize so base and barbarous a Weed, or at least overlove so loathsome a Vanity, by a Volley of Holy Shot Thundered from Mount

Helicon," 1615. Controversialists of that period rejoiced in full-worded titles and in full-blooded praise or abuse.

Deacon, as the title of his book just quoted shows, was very fond of alliteration, and one sentence of his diatribe may be quoted. He warned his readers that tobacco-smoke was "very pernicious unto their bodies, too profluvious for many of their purses, and most pestiferous to the publike State." Much may be forgiven, however, to the introducer of so charming a term of abuse as "profluvious." Deacon's book takes the form of a dialogue, and after nearly 200 pages of argument, in which the unfortunate herb gets no mercy, one of the interlocutors, a trader in tobacco, is so convinced of the iniquity of his trade, and of his own parlous state if he continue therein, that he declares that the two hundred pounds' worth of this "beastly tobacco" which he owns, shall "presently packe to the fire," or else be sent "swimming down the Thames."

Many good folk would seem to have associated smoking with idling. In the rules of the Grammar School at Chigwell, Essex, which was founded in 1629, it is prescribed that "the Master must be a man of sound religion, neither a Papist nor a Puritan, of a grave behaviour, and sober and honest conversation, no tippler or haunter of alehouses, no puffer of tobacco." A worthy Derbyshire man named Campbell, in his will dated 20 October 1616, left all his household goods to his son, "on this condition that yf at any time hereafter, any of his brothers or sisters shall fynd him takeing of tobacco, that then he or she so fynding him, shall have the said goods"--a testamentary arrangement which suggests to the fancy some amusing strategic evasions and manoeuvres on the part of the conditional legatee and his watchful relations.

A converse view of smoking may be seen in Izaak Walton's "Life" of Sir Henry Wotton, who died in 1639. Walton says that Wotton obtained relief to some extent from asthma by leaving off smoking which he had practised "somewhat immoderately"--"as many thoughtful men do ." The italics are mine.

Tobacco, as has been said, was praised as well as abused extravagantly. Much absurdity was written in glorification of the medicinal and therapeutic properties of tobacco, but a more sensible note was struck by some lauders of the weed. Marston wrote in 1607:

Musicke, tobacco, sacke and sleepe,
The tide of sorrow backward keep.

An ingenious lover of his pipe declared ironically in the same year that he had found three bad qualities in tobacco, for it made a man a thief (which meant danger), a good fellow (which meant cost), and a niggard ("the name of which is hateful"). "It makes him a theefe," he continued "for he will steale it from his father; a good fellow, for he will give the smoake to a beggar; a niggard, for he will not part with his box to an Emperor!" A character in one of Chapman's plays, 1606, calls tobacco "the gentleman's saint and the soldier's idol." A little-known bard of 1630--Barten Holiday--wrote a poem of eight stanzas with chorus to each in praise of tobacco, in which he showed with a touch of burlesque that the herb was a musician, a lawyer, a physician, a traveller, a critic, an ignis fatuus, and a whiffler, i.e. a braggart. The first verse may suffice as a specimen:

Tobacco's a musician,
And in a pipe delighteth,
It descends in a close
Through the organ of the nose
With a relish that inviteth.

These are merely a few examples of both the praise and the abuse which were lavished upon tobacco at this early stage in the history of smoking. It would be easy to fill many pages with the like testimonials and denunciations, especially the latter, from writers of the early decades of the seventeenth century. Perhaps the most curious thing in connexion with the immense number of allusions to smoking in the literature of the period is that there is no mention whatever of tobacco or smoking in the plays of William Shakespeare. As Edmund Spenser, in the "Faerie Queene," speaks of

The soveraine weede, divine tobacco,
it may be presumed that he was a smoker.

IV
CAVALIER AND ROUNDHEAD SMOKERS

"A custom lothsome to the eye, hatefull to the Nose,
harmefull to the braine, dangerous to the lungs, and in the
blacke stinking fume thereof, nearest resembling the
horrible Stigian smoke of the pit that is
bottomelesse."--JAMES I, A Counterblaste to Tobacco.

The social history of smoking from the point of view of fashion, during the period covered by this and the next two chapters may be summarized in a sentence. Through the middle of the seventeenth century smoking maintained its hold upon all classes of society, but in the later decades there are distinct signs that the habit was becoming less universal; and it seems pretty clear that by the time of Queen Anne, smoking, though still extensively practised in many classes of society, was to a considerable extent out of vogue among those most amenable to the dictates of Fashion.

It is certain that the armies of the Parliament were great smokers, for the finds of seventeenth-century pipes on the sites of their camps have been numerous. A considerable number of pipes of the Caroline period, with the usual small elongated bowls, were found in 1902 at Chichester, in the course of excavating the foundations of the Old Swan Inn, East Street, for building the present branch of the London and County Bank.

We know also that the Roundhead soldiers smoked in circumstances that did them no credit. In the account of the trial of Charles I, written by Dr. George Bates, principal physician to his Majesty, and to Charles II also, we read that when the sentence of the Court presided over by Bradshaw, condemning the King "to death by severing his Head from his Body," had been read, the soldiers treated the fallen monarch with great indignity and barbarity. They spat on his clothes as he passed by, and even in his face; and they "blew the smoak of Tobacco, a thing which they knew his Majesty hated, in his sacred mouth, throwing their broken Pipes in his way as he passed along."

Time brought its revenges. The dead Protector was not treated too respect-fully by his soldiery. Evelyn, describing Cromwell's "superb funeral," says that the soldiers in the procession were "drinking and taking tobacco in the streets as they went."

Whether the use of tobacco prevailed as generally among the Cavalier forces is less certain; but as King Charles hated the weed, courtiers may have frowned upon its use. One distinguished cavalier, however, either smoked his pipe, or proposed to do so, on a historic occasion. In Markham's "Life of the Great Lord Fairfax" there is a lively account of how the Duke, then Marquis, of Newcastle, with his brother Charles Cavendish, drove in a coach and six to the field of Marston Moor on the afternoon before the battle. His Grace was in a very bad humour. "He applied to Rupert," says Markham, "for orders as to the disposal of his own most noble person, and was told that there would be no battle that night, and that he had better get into his coach and go to sleep, which he accordingly did." But the decision as to battle or no battle did not rest with Prince Rupert. Cromwell attacked the royal army with the most disastrous results to the King's cause. His Grace of Newcastle woke up, left his coach, and fought bravely, being, according to his Duchess, the last to ride off the fatal field, leaving his coach and six behind him.

So far Markham: but according to another account, when Rupert told him that there would be no battle, the Duke betook himself to his coach, "lit his pipe, and making himself very comfortable, fell asleep." The original authority, however, for the whole story is to be found in a paper of notes by Clarendon on the affairs of the North, preserved among his MSS. In this paper Clarendon writes: "The marq. asked the prince what he would do? His highness answered, 'Wee will charge them to-morrow morninge.' My lord asked him whether he were sure the enimy would not fall on them sooner? He answered, 'No'; and the marquisse thereupon going to his coach hard by, and callinge for a pype of tobacco, before he could take it the enimy charged, and instantly all the prince's horse were routed."

Gardiner evidently follows this account, for his version of the story is: "New-castle strolled towards his coach to solace himself with a pipe. Before he had time to take a whiff, the battle had begun." The incident was made the subject of a picture by Ernest Crofts, A.R.A., which was exhibited at the Royal Academy in 1888. It shows the Duke leaning out of his carriage window, with his pipe in his hand.

Among the documents in the possession of the Society of Antiquaries of Scotland there is a letter patent under the great seal of Charles I, in 1634, granted for the purpose of correcting the irregular sales and restraining the immoderate use of tobacco in Scotland. The letter states that tobacco was used on its first introduction as a medicine, but had since been so largely indulged in and was frequently of such bad quality, as not only to injure the health, but deprave the morals of the King's subjects. These were sentiments worthy of King James. Mr. Matthew Livingstone, who has calendared this document, says that the King therein proceeds, in order to prevent such injurious results of the use of tobacco, to appoint Sir James Leslie and Thomas Dalmahoy to enjoy for seven years the sole power of appointing licensed vendors of the commodity. These vendors, after due examination as to their fitness, were to be permitted, on payment of certain compositions and an annual rent in augmentation of the King's revenue, to sell tobacco in small quantities. The letter further directs that the licensees so appointed shall become bound to sell only sound tobacco--an admirable provision, if a trifle difficult to enforce--and to keep good order in their houses and shops. "The latter clause," adds Mr. Livingstone, "would almost suggest that the tobacco was to be sold for consumption on the premises,"--as I have no doubt it was--"and that the smokers were probably in the habit at their symposiums of using, even as they may still, I dare say, other indulgences not so soothing in their effects as the coveted weed"--a suggestion for which there seems little foundation in the clause to which Mr. Livingstone refers.

One inference at least may be fairly drawn, I think, from this document, and that is that smoking was very popular north as well as south of the Tweed.

Tobacco was certainly cheap in Scotland. The following entries are from a MS. account of household expenses kept by the minister of the parish of Eastwood, near Glasgow, the Rev. William Hamilton. They cover two months only and show that the minister was a furious smoker. The prices given are in Scots currency, the pound Scots being worth about twenty pence sterling:

Maii, 1651
It. to Andro Carnduff for 4 pund of Tobacco
L1. 0. 0.
It. to Robert Hamilton Chapman for Tobacco
0. 18. 0.
It. 9 June to my wife to give for sax trenchers
and tobacco
1. 13. 4.
It. 10 June, The sd day for tobacco and stuffes
0. 14. 4.
28 June, It. for tobacco
0. 13. 9.

It may perhaps be interesting to compare with these prices, from which, apparently, it may be inferred that near Glasgow tobacco could be bought for some 5d. a pound, which seems incredibly cheap, the occasional expenditure upon tobacco of a worthy citizen of Exeter some few years earlier. Extracts from the "Financial Diary" of this good man, whose name was John Hayne, and who was an extensive dealer in serges and woollen goods generally, as well as in a smaller degree of cotton goods also, were printed some years ago, with copious annotations, by the late Dr. Brushfield.

In this "Diary," covering the years 1631-43, there are some forty entries concerning the purchase of what is always, save in one case, called "tobacka." These entries give valuable information as to the prices of the two chief kinds of tobacco. One was imported from Spanish America, which up to 1639 Hayne calls "Varinaes," and after that date "Spanish"; the other was imported from English colonies--chiefly from Virginia. The "Varinaes" kind, Dr. Brushfield suggests, was obtained from Varina, near the foot of the range of mountains forming the west boundary of Venezuela, and watered by a branch of the Orinoco River. Hayne also notes the purchase of "Tertudoes" tobacco, but what that may have been I cannot say. From the various entries relating respectively to Varinaes or Spanish tobacco, and to Virginia tobacco, it is clear that the former ranged in price from 8s. to 13s. per lb., while the latter was from 1s. 6d. to 4s. per lb. There is one entry of "perfumed

Tobacka," 10 oz. of which were bought at the very high price of 15s. 6d.

The variations in price of both Spanish and Virginia tobacco were largely due to the frequent changes in the amount of the duty thereon. In 1604 King James I, newly come to the throne, and full of iconoclastic fervour against the weed, raised the duty to 6s. 8d. per lb. in addition to the original duty of 2d. On March 29, 1615, there was a grant to a licensed importer "of the late imposition of 2s. per lb. on tobacco"--which shows that there must have been considerable fluctuation between 1604 and 1615--while in September 1621 the duty stood at 9d. Through James's reign much dissatisfaction was expressed about the importation of Spanish tobacco, and the outcome of this may probably be seen in the proclamations issued by the King in his last two years forbidding "the importation, buying, or selling tobacco which was not of the proper growth of the colonies of Virginia and the Somers Islands." These proclamations were several times confirmed by Charles I, the latest being on January 8, 1631; but they do not seem to have had much effect.

Hayne's "Diary" contains one or two entries relating to smokers' requisites. In September 1639 he spent 2d. on a new spring to his "Tobacka tonges." These were the tongs used for lifting a live coal to light the pipe, to which I have referred on a previous page. On the last day of 1640 Hayne paid "Mr. Drakes man" 1s. 5d. for "6 doz: Tobacka-pipes."

From the various entries in the "Diary" relating to the purchase of tobacco, it seems clear that there was no shop in Exeter devoted specially or exclusively to the sale of the weed. Hayne bought his supplies from four of the leading goldsmiths of the city, who can be identified by the fact that he had dealings with them in their own special wares, also from two drapers, one grocer, and four other tradesmen (on a single occasion each) whose particular occupations are unknown.

But to turn from this worthy Exeter citizen to more famous names: I do not know of any good evidence as to whether or not Cromwell smoked, although he is said to have taken an occasional pipe while considering the offer of the crown, but John Milton certainly did. The account of how the blind poet passed his days, after his retirement from public office, was first told by his contemporary Richardson, and has since been repeated by all his biographers. His placid day ended early. The poet took his frugal supper at eight o'clock, and at nine, having smoked a pipe and drunk a glass of water, he went to bed. Apparently this modest allowance of a daily evening pipe was the extent of Milton's indulgence in tobacco. He knew nothing of what most smokers regard as the best pipe of the day--the after-breakfast pipe.

It is somewhat singular that the Puritans, who denounced most amusements and pleasures, and who frowned upon most of the occupations or diversions that make for gaiety and the enjoyment of life, did not, as Puritans, denounce the use of tobacco. One or two of their writers abused it roundly; but these were not representative of Puritan feeling on the subject. The explanation doubtless is that the practice of smoking was so very general and so much a matter of course among men of all ranks and of all opinions, that the mouths of Puritans were closed, so to speak, by their own pipes. A precisian, however, could take his tobacco with a difference. The seventeenth-century diarist, Abraham de la Pryme, says that he had heard of a Presbyterian minister who was so precise that "he would not as much as take a pipe of tobacco before that he had first sayed grace over it." George Wither, one of the most noteworthy of the poets who took the side of the Parliament, was confined in Newgate after the Restoration, and found comfort in his pipe.

Some of the Puritan colonists in America took a strong line on the subject. Under the famous "Blue Laws" of 1650 it was ordered by the General Court of Connecticut that no one under twenty-one was to smoke--"nor any other that hath not already accustomed himself to the use thereof." And no smoker could enjoy his pipe unless he obtained a doctor's certificate that tobacco would be "usefull for him, and allso that he hath received a lycense from the Courte for the same." But the unhappy smoker having passed the doctor and obtained his licence was still harassed by restrictions, for it was ordered that no man within the colony, after the publication of the order, should take any tobacco publicly "in the streett, highwayes, or any barn-yardes, or uppon training dayes, in any open places, under the penalty of six-pence for each offence against this order." The ingenuities of petty tyranny are ineffable. It is said that these "Blue Laws" are not authentic; but if they are not literally true, they are certainly well invented, for most of them can be paralleled and illustrated by laws and regulations of undoubted authenticity.

Mrs. Alice Morse Earle, in her interesting book, abounding in curious information, on "The Sabbath in Puritan New England," says that the use of tobacco "was absolutely forbidden under any circumstances on the Sabbath within two miles of the meeting-house, which (since at that date all the houses were clustered round the church-green) was equivalent to not smoking it at all on the Lord's Day, if the law were obeyed. But wicked backsliders existed, poor slaves of habit, who were in Duxbury fixed 10s. for each offence, and in Portsmouth, not only were fined, but to their shame be it told, set as jail-birds in the Portsmouth cage. In Sandwich and in Boston the fine for 'drinking tobacco in the meeting-house' was 5s. for each drink, which I take to mean chewing tobacco rather than smoking it; many men were fined for thus drinking, and solacing the weary hours, though doubtless they were as sly and kept themselves as unobserved as possible. Four Yarmouth men-- old sea-dogs, perhaps, who loved their pipe--were in 1687 fined 4s. each for smoking tobacco around the end of the meeting-house. Silly, ostrich-brained Yarmouth men! to fancy to escape detection by hiding around the corner of the church; and to think that the tithing-man had no nose when he was so Argus-eyed."

On weekdays many New England Puritans probably smoked as their friends in old England did. A contemporary painting of a group of Puritan divines over the mantelpiece of Parson Lowell, of Newbury, shows them well provided with punch-bowl and drinking-cups, tobacco and pipes. One parson, the Rev. Mr. Bradstreet, of the First Church of Charlestown, was very unconventional in his attire. He seldom wore a coat, "but generally appeared in a plaid gown, and was always seen with a pipe in his mouth." John Eliot, the noble preacher and missionary to the Indians, warmly denounced both the wearing of wigs and the smoking of tobacco. But his denunciations were ineffectual in both matters--heads continued to be adorned with curls of foreign growth, and pipe-smoke continued to ascend.

In this country tobacco is said to have invaded even the House of Commons itself. Mr. J.H. Burn, in his "Descriptive Catalogue of London Tokens," writes: "About the middle of the seventeenth century it was ordered: That no member of the House do presume to smoke tobacco in the gallery or at the table of the House sitting as Committees." I do not know what the authority for this order may be, but there is no doubt that smoking was practised in the precincts of the House. In "Mercurius Pragmaticus," December 19-26, 1648, the writer says on December 20, speaking of the excluded members: "Col. Pride standing sentinell at the door, denyed entrance, and caused them to retreat into the Lobby where they used to drink ale and tobacco."

There is a curious entry in Thomas Burton's diary of the proceedings of Cromwell's Parliament, which suggests that there may then have been the luxury of a members' smoking-room. Burton was a member of the Parliaments of Oliver and Richard Cromwell from 1656 to 1659, and made a practice--for which historical students have been and are much his debtors--of taking notes of the debates as he sat in the House. Members sometimes objected to and protested against this note-taking, but Burton quietly went on using his pencil, and though his summaries of speeches are often difficult to follow, argument and sense suffering by compression, he has preserved much very valuable matter. Referring to a debate on January 7, 1656-57, on an attempt to go behind the previously passed Act of Oblivion, the diarist records that "Sir John Reynolds had numbered the House, and said at rising there were 220 at the least, besides tobacconists." This can only mean that there were at least 220 members actually present in the House when it rose, not counting the "tobacconists" or smokers, who were enjoying their pipes, not in the Chamber itself, but in some conveniently adjoining place, which may have been a room for the purpose, or may simply have been the lobby referred to above in the extract from "Mercurius Pragmaticus."

It seems likely that Richard Cromwell was a smoker. In 1689, long after he had retired into private life and had ample leisure for blowing clouds, he sent to a friend a "Boxe of Tobacco," which was described as "A.J. Bod (den's) ... best Virginnea." In a letter to his daughter Elizabeth, dated 21 January 1705, there is a reference to this same dealer, whom he describes as "Adam Bodden, Bacconist in George Yard, Lumber [Lombard] Street." The allusion is worth noting as a very early instance of the colloquial trick of abbreviation familiar in later days in such forms as "baccy" and "bacca" and their compounds.

V
SMOKING IN THE RESTORATION PERIOD

The Indian weed withered quite
Green at noon, cut down at night,
Shows thy decay--
All flesh is hay:
Thus think, then drink tobacco.
GEORGE WITHER (1588-1667).

The year 1660 that restored Charles II to his throne, restored a gaiety and brightness, not to say frivolity of tone, that had long been absent from English life. The following song in praise of tobacco, taken from a collection which was printed in 1660, is touched with the spirit of the time; though it is really founded on, and to no small extent taken from, some verses in praise of tobacco written by Samuel Rowlands in his "Knave of Clubs," 1611:

To feed on flesh is gluttony,
It maketh men fat like swine;
But is not he a frugal man
That on a leaf can dine?

He needs no linnen for to foul
His fingers' ends to wipe,
That has his kitchin in a box,
And roast meat in a pipe.

The cause wherefore few rich men's sons
Prove disputants in schools,
Is that their fathers fed on flesh,
And they begat fat fools.

This fulsome feeding cloggs the brain
And doth the stomach choak
But he's a brave spark that can dine
With one light dish of smoak.

There is nothing to show that King Charles smoked, nor what his personal attitude towards tobacco may have been.

His Majesty was pleased, however, in a letter to Cambridge University, officially to condemn smoking by parsons, as at the same time he condemned the practice of wig-wearing and of sermon-reading by the clergy. But the royal frown was without effect. Wigs soon covered nearly every clerical head from the bench of bishops downwards; and it is very doubtful indeed whether a single parson put his pipe out.

Clouds were blown under archiepiscopal roofs. At Lambeth Palace one Sunday in February 1672 John Eachard, the author of the famous book or tract on "The Contempt of the Clergy," 1670, which Macaulay turned to such account, dined with Archbishop Sheldon. He sat at the lower end of the table between the archbishop's two chaplains; and when dinner was finished, Sheldon, we are told, retired to his withdrawing-room, while Eachard went with the chaplains and another convive to their lodgings "to drink and smoak."

If the restored king did not himself smoke, tobacco was far from unknown at the Palace of Whitehall. We get a curious glimpse of one aspect of life there in the picture which Lilly, the notorious astrologer, paints in his story of his arrest in January 1661. He was taken to Whitehall at night, and kept in a large room with some sixty other prisoners till daylight, when he was transferred to the guardroom, which, he says, "I thought to be hell; some therein were sleeping, others swearing, others smoking tobacco. In the chimney of the room I believe there was two bushels of broken tobacco pipes, almost half one load of ashes." What would the king's grandfather, the author of the "Counterblaste," have said, could he have imagined such a spectacle within the palace walls?

General Monk, to whom Charles II owed so much, is said to have indulged in the unpleasant habit of chewing tobacco, and to have been imitated by others; but the practice can never have been common.

Tobacco was still the symbol of good-fellowship. Winstanley, who was an enemy of what he called "this Heathenish Weed," and who thought the "folly" of smoking might never have spread so much if stringent "means of prevention" had been exercised, yet had to declare in 1660 that "Tobacco it self is by few taken now as medicinal, it is grown a good-fellow, and fallen from a Physician to a Complement. 'He's no good-fellow that's without ... burnt Pipes, Tobacco, and his Tinder-Box.'"

At the time of the Restoration tobacco-boxes which were considered suitable to the occasion were made in large numbers. The outside of the lid bore a portrait of the Royal Martyr; within the lid was a picture of the restored king, His Majesty King Charles II; while on the inside of the bottom of the box was a representation of Oliver Cromwell leaning against a post, a gallows-tree over his head, and about his neck a halter tied to the tree, while beside him was pictured the devil, wide-mouthed. Another form of memorial tobacco-box is described in an advertisement in the London Gazette of September 15, 1687. This was a silver box which had either been "taken out of the Bull's Head Tavern, Cheapside, or left in a Hackney Coach." It was "ingraved on the Lid with a Coat of Arms, etc., and a Medal of Charles the First fastened to the inside of the Lid, and engraved on the inside 'to Jacob Smith it doth belong, at the Black Lyon in High Holborn, date August 1671.'"

Smokers of the period were often curious in tobacco-boxes. Mr. Richard Stapley, gentleman, of Twineham, Sussex, whose diary is full of curious information, was presented in 1691 by his friend Mr. John Hill with a "tobacco-box made of tortoise." Seven years earlier Stapley had sold to Hill his silver tobacco-box for 10s. in cash--the rest of the value of the box, he noted, "I freely forgave him for writing at our first commission for me, and for copying of answers and ye like in our law concerns; so yt I reckon I have as good as 30s. for my box: 5s. he gave me, and 5s. more he promised to pay me ... and I had his steel box with the bargain, and full of smoake." Apparently Mr. Hill's secretarial labours were valued at 20s. This same Sussex squire bought a pound of tobacco in December 1685 for 20d., which seems decidedly cheap, and in the following year a 5 lb. box for 7s. 6d.--which was cheaper still.

A Sussex rector, the Rev. Giles Moore, of Horsted Keynes, in 1656 and again in 1662, paid 1s. for two ounces of tobacco, i.e. at the rate of 8s. per lb. Presumably the rector bought the more expensive Spanish tobacco and the squire the cheaper Virginian. At the annual parish feast held at St. Bride's, Fleet Street, London, on May 24, 1666, the expenses included 3d. for tobacco for twenty or more adults. This too was doubtless Virginian or colonial tobacco. The North Elmham Church Accounts (Norfolk) for 1673 show that 12s. 4d. was paid for "Butter, cheese, Bread, Cakes, Beere and Tobacco and Tobacco Pipes at the goeing of the Rounds of the Towne." On the occasion of a similar perambulation of the parish boundaries in 1714-15 the churchwardens paid for beer, pipes and tobacco, cakes and wine. The account-books of the church and parish of St. Stephen, Norwich, for 1696-97 show 2s. as the price of a pound of tobacco. These entries, and many others of similar import, show that at feasts and at social and convivial gatherings of all kinds, tobacco maintained its ascendancy. Pipes and tobacco were included in the usual provision for city feasts, mayoral and other; and smoking was made a particular feature of the Lord Mayor's Show of 1672. A contemporary pamphleteer says that in the Show of that year were "two extreme great giants, each of them at least 15 foot high, that do sit, and are drawn by horses in two several chariots, moving, talking, and taking tobacco as they ride along, to the great admiration and delight of all the spectators." Among the guests at a wedding in London in 1683 were the Lord Mayor, Sheriff and Aldermen of the City, the Lord Chief Justice--the afterwards notorious Jeffreys-- and other "bigwigs." Evelyn records with grave disapproval that "these great men spent the rest of the afternoon till 11 at night, in drinking healths, taking tobacco, and talking much beneath the gravity of judges, who had but a day or two before condemned Mr. Algernon Sidney."

Although smoking was general among parsons, yet attacks on tobacco were occasionally heard from pulpits. A Lancashire preacher named Thomas Jollie, who was one of the ministers ejected from Church livings by the Act of Uniformity, 1662, has left a manuscript diary relating to his religious work. In it, under date 1687, he mentions that he had spoken "against the inordinate affection to and the immoderate use of tobacco which did caus much trouble in some of my hearers and some reformation did follow." He then goes on to record two remarkable examples of such "reformation"--examples, he says, "which did stirr me up in that case more than ordinary. The one I had from my reverend Brother Mr. Robert Whittaker, concerning a professor [i.e. a person who professed to have been "converted"] who could not follow his calling without his pipe in his mouth, but that text Isaiah 55, 2, coming into his mind hee layd aside his taking of tobacco. The other instance was of a profane person living nigh Haslingdon (who was but poor) and took up his time in the trade of smoking and also spent what should reliev his poor family. This man dreamed that he was taking tobacco, and that the devill stood by him filling one pipe upon another for him. In the morning hee fell to his old cours notwith-standing; thinking it was but a dream: but when hee came to take his pipe, hee had such an apprehension that the devill did indeed stand by him and doe the office as hee dreamed that hee was struck speechless for a time and when hee came to him-self hee threw his tobacco in the fire and his pipes at the walls; resolving never to meddle more with it: soe much money as was formerly wasted by the week in to serving his family afterward weekly."

Among the many medicinal virtues attributed to tobacco was its supposed value as a preservative from contagion at times of plague. Hearne, the antiquary, writing early in 1721, said that he had been told that in the Great Plague of London of 1665 none of those who kept tobacconists' shops suffered from it, and this belief no doubt enhanced the medical reputation of the weed. I have also seen it stated that during the cholera epidemics of 1831, 1849, and 1866 not one London tobacconist died from that disease; but good authority for the statement seems to be lacking. Hutton, in his "History of Derby," says that when that town was visited by the plague in 1665, that at the "Headless-cross ... the market-people, having their mouths primed with tobacco as a preservative, brought their provisions.... It was observed, that this cruel affliction never attempted the premises of a tobacconist, a tanner or a shoe-maker." Whatever ground there may have been for the belief in the prophylactic effect of smoking, there can be no doubt that in the seventeenth century it was firmly held. Howell in one of his "Familiar Letters" dated January 1, 1646, says that the smoke of tobacco is "one of the wholesomest sents that is against all contagious airs, for it overmasters all other smells, as King James they say found true, when being once a hunting, a showr of rain drave him into a Pigsty for shelter, wher he caus'd a pipe full to Be taken of purpose." But here Mr. Howell is certainly drawing the long-bow. One cannot imagine the author of the "Counterblaste" countenancing the use of tobacco under any circumstances.

At the time of the Great Plague all kinds of nostrums were sold and recommended as preservatives or as cures. Most of these perished with the occasion that called them forth; but the names of some have been preserved in a rare quarto tract which was published in the Plague year, 1665, entitled "A Brief Treatise of the Nature, Causes, Signes, Preservation from and Cure of the Pestilence," "collected by W. Kemp, Mr. of Arts." In the list of devices for purifying infected air it is stated that "The American Silver-weed, or Tobacco, is very excellent for this purpose, and an excellent defence against bad air, being smoked in a pipe, either by itself, or with Nutmegs shred, and Rew Seeds mixed with it, especially if it be nosed"--which, I suppose, means if the smoke be exhaled through the nose--"for it cleanseth the air, and choaketh, suppresseth and disperseth any venomous vapour." Mr. Kemp warms to his subject and proceeds with a whole-hearted panegyric that must be quoted in full: "It hath singular and contrary effects, it is good to warm one being cold, and will cool one being hot. All ages, all Sexes, all Constitutions, Young and Old, Men and Women, the Sanguine, the Cholerick, the Melancholy, the phlegmatick, take it without any manifest inconvenience, it quencheth thirst, and yet will make one more able, and fit to drink; it abates hunger, and yet will get one a good stomach; it is agreeable with mirth or sadness, with feasting and with fasting; it will make one rest that wants sleep, and will keep one waking that is drowsie; it hath an offensive smell to some, and is more desirable than any perfume to others; that it is a most excellent preservative, both experience and reason do teach; it corrects the air by Fumigation, and it avoids corrupt humours by Salivation; for when one takes it either by Chewing it in the leaf, or Smoaking it in the pipe, the humors are drawn and brought from all parts of the body, to the stomach, and from thence rising up to the mouth of the Tobacconist, as to the helme of a Sublimatory, are voided and spitten out."

When plague was abroad even children were compelled to smoke. At the time of the dreadful visitation of 1665 all the boys at Eton were obliged to smoke in school every morning. One of these juvenile smokers, a certain Tom Rogers, years afterwards declared to Hearne, the Oxford antiquary, that he never was whipped so much in his life as he was one morning for not smoking. Times have changed at Eton since this anti-tobacconist martyr received his whipping. It is sometimes stated that at this time smoking was generally practised in schools, and that at a stated hour each morning lessons were laid aside, and masters and scholars alike produced their pipes and proceeded to smoke tobacco. But I know of no authority for this wider statement; it seems to have grown out of Hearne's record of the practice at Eton.

The belief in the prophylactic power of tobacco was, however, very generally held. When Mr. Samuel Pepys on June 7, 1665, for the first time saw several houses marked with the ominous red cross, and the words "Lord, have mercy upon us" chalked upon the doors, he felt so ill at ease that he was obliged to buy some roll tobacco to smell and chew. There is nothing to show that Pepys even smoked, which considering his proficiency in the arts of good-fellowship, is perhaps a little surprising. Defoe, in his fictitious but graphic "Journal of the Plague Year in London," says that the sexton of one of the London parishes, who personally handled a large number of the victims, never had the distemper at all, but lived about twenty years after it, and was sexton of the parish to the time of his death. This man, according to Defoe, "never used any preservative against the infection other than holding garlic and rue in his mouth, and smoking tobacco."

When excavations were in progress early in 1901, preparatory to the construction of Kingsway and Aldwych, they included the removal of bodies from the burying-grounds of St. Clement Danes and St. Mary-le-Strand; and among the bones were found a couple of the curious tobacco-pipes called "plague-pipes," because they are supposed to have been used as a protection against infection by those whose office it was to bury the dead. These pipes have been dug up from time to time in numbers so large that one antiquary, Mr. H. Syer Cuming, has ventured to infer that "almost every person who ventured from home invoked the protection of tobacco."

These seventeenth-century pipes were largely made in Holland of pipe-clay imported from England--to the disgust and loss of English pipe-makers. In 1663 the Company of Tobacco-Pipe Makers petitioned Parliament "to forbid the export of tobacco pipe clay, since by the manufacture of pipes in Holland their trade is much damaged." Further, they asked for "the confirmation of their charter of government so as to empower them to regulate abuses, as many persons engage in the trade without licence." The Company's request was granted; but in the next year they again found it necessary to come to Parliament, showing "the great improvement in their trade since their incorporation, 17 James I, and their threatened ruin because cooks, bakers, and ale-house keepers and others make pipes, but so unskilfully that they are brought into disesteem; they request to be comprehended in the Statute of Labourers of 5 Elizabeth, so that none may follow the trade who have not been apprentices seven years."

Tobacco-pipe making was a flourishing industry at this period and throughout the seventeenth and following century in most of the chief provincial towns and cities as well as in London.

"Old English 'clays,'" says Mr. T.P. Cooper, "are exceedingly interesting, as most of them are branded with the maker's initials. Monograms and designs were stamped or moulded upon the bowls and on the stems, but more generally upon the spur or flat heel of the pipe. Many pipes display on the heels various forms of lines, hatched and milled, which were perhaps the earliest marks of identification adopted by the pipe-makers. In a careful examination of the monograms we are able to identify the makers of certain pipes found in quantities at various places, by reference to the freeman and burgess rolls and parish registers. During the latter half of the seventeenth century English pipes were presented by colonists in America to the Indians; they subsequently became valuable as objects of barter or part purchase value in exchange for land. In 1677 one hundred and twenty pipes and one hundred Jew's harps were given for a strip of country near Timber Creek, in New Jersey. William Penn, the founder of Pennsylvania, purchased a tract of land, and 300 pipes were included in the articles given in the exchange."

The French traveller, Sorbiere, who visited London in 1663, declared that the English were naturally lazy and spent half their time in taking tobacco. They smoked after meals, he observed, and conversed for a long time. "There is scarce a day passes," he wrote, "but a Tradesman goes to the Ale-house or Tavern to smoke with some of his Friends, and therefore Public Houses are numerous here, and Business goes on but slowly in the Shops"; but, curiously enough, he makes no mention of coffee-houses. A little later they were too common and too much frequented to be overlooked. An English writer on thrift in 1676 said that it was customary for a "mechanic tradesman" to go to the coffee-house or ale-house in the morning to drink his morning's draught, and there he would spend twopence and consume an hour in smoking and talking, spending several hours of the evening in similar fashion.

Country gentlemen smoked just as much as town mechanics and tradesmen. In 1688 Hervey, afterwards Earl of Bristol, wrote to Mr. Thomas Cullum, of Haw-sted Place, desiring "to be remembered by the witty smoakers of Hawsted." A later Cullum, Sir John, published in 1784 a "History and Antiquities of Hawsted," and in describing Hawsted Place, which was rebuilt about 1570, says that there was a small apartment called the smoking-room--"a name," he says, "it acquired probably soon after it was built; and which it retained with good reason, as long as it stood." I should like to know on what authority Sir John Cullum could have made the as-sertion that the room was called the smoking-room from so early a date as the end of the sixteenth century. No mention in print of a smoking-room has been found for the purposes of the Oxford Dictionary earlier than 1689. In Shadwell's "Bury Fair" of that date Lady Fantast says to her husband, Mr. Oldwit, who loves to tell of his early meetings with Ben Jonson and other literary heroes of a bygone day, "While all the Beau Monde, as my daughter says, are with us in the drawing-room, you have none but ill-bred, witless drunkards with you in your smoking-room." As Mr. Oldwit himself, in another scene of the same play, says to his friends, "We'll into my smoking-room and sport about a brimmer," there was probably some ex-cuse for his wife's remark. These country smoking-rooms were known in later days as stone-parlours, the floor being flagged for safety's sake; and the "stone-parlour" in many a squire's house was the scene of much conviviality, including, no doubt, abundant smoking.

The arrival of coffee and the establishment of coffee-houses opened a new field for the victories of tobacco. The first house was opened in St. Michael's Alley, Corn-hill, in 1652. Others soon followed, and in a short time the new beverage had cap-tured the town, and coffee-houses had been opened in every direction. They sold many things besides coffee, and served a variety of purposes, but primarily they were temples of talk and good-fellowship. The buzz of conversation and the smoke of tobacco alike filled the rooms which were the forerunners of the club-houses of a much later day.

VI
SMOKING UNDER KING WILLIAM III
AND QUEEN ANNE

Hail! social pipe--thou foe of care,
Companion of my elbow-chair;
As forth thy curling fumes arise,
They seem an evening sacrifice--
An offering to my Maker's praise,
For all His benefits and grace.
　　　SIR SAMUEL GARTH (1660-1718).

After King William III was settled on the throne the sum of L600,000 was paid to the Dutch from the English exchequer for money advanced in connexion with his Majesty's expedition, and this amount was paid off by tobacco duties. Granger long ago remarked that most of the eminent divines and bishops of the day contributed very practically to the payment of this revolutionary debt by their large consumption of tobacco. He mentions Isaac Barrow, Dr. Barlow of Lincoln, who was as regular in smoking tobacco as at his meals, and had a high opinion of its virtues, Dr. Aldrich, "and other celebrated persons who flourished about this time, and gave much into that practice." One of the best known of these celebrated persons was Gilbert Burnet, Bishop of Salisbury from 1689, and historian of his own times. He had the reputation of being an inveterate smoker, and was caricatured with a long clay stuck through the brim of the shovel hat, on the breadth of which King William once made remark. The bishop replied that the hat was of a shape suited to his dignity, whereupon the King caustically said, "I hope that the hat won't turn your head."

Thackeray pictures Dryden as sitting in his great chair at Will's Coffee-house, Russell Street, Covent Garden, tobacco-pipe in hand; but there is no evidence that Dryden smoked. The snuff-box was his symbol of authority. Budding wits thought themselves highly distinguished if they could obtain the honour of being allowed to take a pinch from it. Of Dr. Aldrich, who was Dean of Christ Church, Oxford, and who wrote a curious "Catch not more difficult to sing than diverting to hear, to be sung by four men smoking their pipes," an anecdote has often been related, which illustrates his devotion to the weed. A bet was made by one undergraduate and taken by another, that at whatever time, however early, the Dean might be visited in his own den, he would be found smoking. As soon as the bet had been made the Dean was visited. The pair explained the reason for their call, when Aldrich, who must have been a good-tempered man, said, "Your friend has lost: I am not smoking, only filling my pipe."

John Philips, the author of "Cyder" and the "Splendid Shilling," was an undergraduate at Christ Church, during Aldrich's term of office, and no doubt learned to smoke in an atmosphere so favourable to tobacco. In his "Splendid Shilling," which dates from about 1700, Philips says of the happy man with a shilling in his pocket:

Meanwhile, he smokes, and laughs at merry tale,
Or Pun ambiguous or Conundrum quaint.

But the poor shillingless wretch can only

 doze at home
In garret vile, and with a warming puff
Regale chill'd fingers; or from tube as black
As winter-chimney, or well-polish'd jet,
Exhale Mundungus, ill-perfuming scent.

The miserable creature, though without a shilling, yet possessed a well-coloured "clay."

It is significant that the writer of a life of Philips, which was prefixed to an edition of his poems which was published in 1762, after mentioning that smoking was common at Oxford in the days of Aldrich, says apologetically, "It is no wonder therefore that he [Philips] fell in with the general taste ... he has descended to sing its praises in more than one place." By 1762, as we shall see, smoking was quite unfashionable, and consequently it was necessary to explain how it was that a poet could "descend" so low as to sing the praises of tobacco.

Other well-known men of the late seventeenth century were "tobacconists" in the old sense of the word. Sir Isaac Newton is said to have smoked immoderately; and a familiar anecdote represents him as using for the purposes of a tobacco-stopper, in a fit of absent-mindedness, the little finger of a lady sitting beside him, whom he admired, but the truth of this legend is open to doubt. Thomas Hobbes, who lived to be ninety (1588-1679), was accustomed to dine at 11 o'clock, after which he smoked a pipe and then lay down and took a nap of about half an hour. No doubt he would have attributed the length of his days to the regularity of his habits. Izaak Walton, who also lived to be ninety, as the lover of the placid and contemplative life deserved to do, loved his pipe, though he seldom mentions smoking in the "Compleat Angler." Sir Samuel Garth, poet and physician, once known to fame as the author of "The Dispensary," was another pipe-lover, as is shown by his verses quoted at the head of this chapter. Dudley, the fourth Lord North, began to smoke in 1657, and, says Dr. Jessopp, "the habit grew upon him, the frequent entries for pipes and tobacco showing that he became more and more addicted to this indulgence. Probably it afforded him some solace in the dreadful malady from which he suffered so long."

Even the staid Quakers smoked. George Fox's position in regard to tobacco was curious. He did not smoke himself; but on one occasion he was offered a pipe by a jesting youth who thought thereby to shock so saintly a person. Fox says in his "Journal," "I lookt upon him to bee a forwarde bolde lad: and tobacco I did not take: butt ... I saw hee had a flashy empty notion of religion: soe I took his pipe and putt it to my mouth and gave it to him again to stoppe him lest his rude tongue should say I had not unity with ye creation." The incident is curious, but testifies to Fox's tolerance and breadth of outlook.

Many of his followers smoked, sometimes apparently to such an extent as to cause scandal among their brethren. The following is an entry in the minutes of the Friends' Monthly Meeting at Hardshaw, Lancashire: "14th of 4th mo. 1691. It being considered that the too frequent use of smoking Tobacco is inconsistent with friends holy profession, it is desired that such as have occasion to make use thereof take it privately, neither too publicly in their own houses, nor by the highways, streets, or in alehouses or elsewhere, tending to the abetting the common excess." Another Lancashire Monthly Meeting, Penketh, under date "18th 8th mo. 1691" suggested that Friends were "not to smoke during their labour or occupation, but to leave their work and take it privately"--a suggestion which clearly proceeded from non-smokers. The smug propriety of these recommendations to enjoy a smoke in private is delightful.

At the Quarterly Meeting of Aberdeen Friends in 1692 a "weighty paper containing several heads of solid advyces and Counsells to friends" sent by Irish Quakers, was read. These counsels abound with amusingly prim suggestions. Among them is the warning to "take heed of being overcome with strong drink or tobacco, which many by custome are brought into bondag to the creature." The Aberdeen Friends themselves a little later were greatly concerned at the increasing indulgence in "superfluous apparell and in vain recreations among the young ones"; and in 1698 they issued a paper dealing in great detail with matters of dress and deportment. Among a hundred other things treated with minutest particularity, the desire is expressed that "all Idle and needless Smoaking of Tobacco be forborn."

William Penn did not like tobacco and was often annoyed by it in America. Clarkson, his biographer, relates that on one occasion Penn called to see some old friends at Burlington, who had been smoking, but who, in consideration for his feelings, had put their pipes away. Penn smelt the tobacco, and noticing that the pipes were concealed, said, "Well, friends, I am glad that you are at last ashamed of your old practice." "Not entirely so," replied one of the company, "but we preferred laying down our pipes to the danger of offending a weaker brother."

Many of the tobacco-boxes used in the latter part of the seventeenth century were imported from Holland. They were long or oval and were usually made of brass. They can be easily identified by their engraved subjects and Dutch inscriptions. An example in the Colchester Museum is made of copper and brass, with embossed designs and inscriptions, representing commerce, &c., on the base and lid. It has engraved on the sides the name and address of its owner--"Barnabas Barker,

Wyvenhoe, Essex." The similar boxes later made in England usually had embossed ornamentation.

The local authorities in our eastern counties seem to have had some curious ideas of their own as to where tobacco should or should not be smoked. In a previous chapter we have seen that at Norwich, ale-house keepers were fined for permitting smoking in their houses. At Methwold, Suffolk, the folk improved upon this. The court-books of the manor of Methwold contain the following entry made at a court held on October 4, 1695: "We agree that any person that is taken smoakeinge tobacco in the street shall forfitt one shillinge for every time so taken, and itt shall be lawfull for the petty constabbles to distrane for the same for to be putt to the uses abovesaid [i.e. "to the use of the town"]. Wee present Nicholas Baker for smoakeinge in the street, and doe amerce him 1s." The same rule is repeated at courts held in the years 1696 and 1699, but no other fine is mentioned at any subsequent courts. The good folk at Methwold may have been adepts at petty tyranny, but such an absurd regulation must soon have become a dead letter. While we are in the eastern counties we may note that in 1694 there died at Ely an apothecary named Henry Crofts, who owned, among some other unusual items in his inventory, casks of brandy and tobacco, which shows that even at that date, when regular tobacconists' shops for the sale of tobacco had long been common, the old business connexion between apothecaries and tobacco still occasionally existed.

The clay pipes called "aldermen," with longer stems than their predecessors, tipped with glaze, came into use towards the end of the seventeenth century. They must not be confused with the much longer "churchwarden" or "yard of clay" which was not in vogue till the early years of the nineteenth century.

Towards the close of the seventeenth century signs may be detected of some waning in the universal popularity of tobacco. There are hints of change in the records of City and other companies. Tobacco had always figured prominently in the provision for trade feasts. In 1651 the Chester Company of Barbers, Surgeons, Wax and Tallow Chandlers--a remarkably comprehensive organization--paid for "Sack beere and Tobacco" at the Talbot on St. Luke's Day, October 18, on the occasion of a dinner given to the Company by one Richard Walker; and similar expenditure was common among both London and provincial Companies. The court-books of the Skinners Company of London show that in preparation for their annual Election Dinner in 1694, the cook appeared before the court and produced a bill of fare which, with some alterations, was agreed to. The butler then appeared and undertook to provide knives, salt, pepper-pots, glasses, sauces, &c., "and everything needfull for L7. and if he gives content then to have L8. he provides all things but pipes, Tobacco, candles and beer"--which apparently fell to the lot of some other caterer.

But so early as 1655 there is a sign of change of custom--a change, that is, in the direction of restricting and limiting the hitherto unbounded freedom granted to the use of tobacco. The London Society of Apothecaries on August 15, 1655, held a meeting for the election of a Master and an Upper Warden; and from the minutes of this meeting we learn that by general consent it was forbidden henceforward to smoke in the Court Room while dining or sitting, under penalty of half a crown.

The more fashionable folk of the Restoration Era and later began to leave off if not to disdain the smoking-habit. Up to about 1700 smoking had been permitted in the public rooms at Bath, but when Nash then took charge, tobacco was banished. Public or at least fashionable taste had begun to change, and Nash correctly interpreted and led it. Sorbiere, who has been quoted in the previous chapter, remarked in 1663 that "People of Quality" did not use tobacco so much as others; and towards the end of the century and in Queen Anne's time the tendency was for tobacco to go out of fashion. This did not much affect its general use; but the tendency--with exceptions, no doubt--was to restrict the use of tobacco to the clergy, to country squires, to merchants and tradesmen and to the humbler ranks of society--to limit it, in short, to the middle and lower classes of the social commonwealth as then organized. In the extraordinary record of inanity which Addison printed as the diary of a citizen in the Spectator of March 4, 1712, the devotion of the worthy retired tradesman to tobacco is emphasized. This is the kind of thing: "Monday ... Hours 10, 11 and 12 Smoaked three Pipes of Virginia ... one o'clock in the afternoon, chid Ralph for mislaying my Tobacco-Box.... Wednesday ... From One to Two Smoaked a Pipe and a half.... Friday ... From Four to Six. Went to the Coffee-house. Met Mr. Nisby there. Smoaked several Pipes."

There was indeed no diminution of tobacco-smoke in the coffee-houses. A visitor from abroad, Mr. Muralt, a Swiss gentleman, writing about 1696, said that character could be well studied at the coffee-houses. He was probably not a smoker himself, for he goes on to say that in other respects the coffee-houses are "loathsome, full of smoke like a guardroom, and as much crowded." He further observed that it was common to see the clergy of London in coffee-houses and even in taverns, with pipes in their mouths. A native witness of about the same date, Ned Ward, writes sneeringly in his "London Spy," 1699, of the interior of the coffee-house. He saw "some going, some coming, some scribbling, some talking, some drinking, some smoking, others jingling; and the whole room stinking of tobacco, like a Dutch scoot, or a boatswain's cabin.... We each of us stuck in our mouths a pipe of sotweed, and now began to look about us." Ward's contemporary, Tom Brown, took a different tone: he wrote of "Tobacco, Cole and the Protestant Religion, the three great blessings of life!"--as strange a jumble as one could wish for.

Even children seem to have smoked sometimes in the coffee-houses. Ralph Thoresby, the Leeds antiquary, tells a strange story. He declares that, one evening which he spent with his brother at Garraway's Coffee-house, February 20, 1702, he was surprised to see his brother's "sickly child of three years old fill its pipe of tobacco and smoke it as audfarandly as a man of three score; after that a second and a third pipe without the least concern, as it is said to have done above a year ago." A child of two years of age smoking three pipes in succession is a picture a little difficult to accept as true. As this is the only reference to tobacco in the whole of his "Diary," it is not likely that Thoresby was himself a smoker.

At the coffee-house entrance was the bar presided over by the predecessors of the modern barmaids--grumbled at in a Spectator as "idols," who there received homage from their admirers, and who paid more attention to customers who flirted with them than to more sober-minded visitors. They are described by Tom Brown as "a charming Phillis or two, who invited you by their amorous glances into their smoaky territories." Admission cost little. There you might see--

Grave wits, who, spending farthings four,
Sit, smoke, and warm themselves an hour.

The allusions in the Spectator *to smoking in the coffee-houses are frequent. "Sometimes," says Addison, in his title character in the first number of the paper, "sometimes I smoak a pipe at Child's and whilst I seem attentive to nothing but the* Post-man, over-hear the conversation of every table in the room." And here is a vignette of coffee-house life in 1714 from No. 568 of the Spectator: "I was yesterday in a coffee-house not far from the Royal Exchange, where I observed three persons in close conference over a pipe of tobacco; upon which, having filled one for my own use, I lighted it at the little wax candle that stood before them; and after having thrown in two or three whiffs amongst them, sat down and made one of the company. I need not tell my reader, that lighting a man's pipe at the same candle is looked upon among brother-smoakers as an overture to conversation and friendship." From the very beginning smoking has induced and fostered a spirit of comradeship.

Sir Roger de Coverley, as a typical country squire, was naturally a smoker. He presented his friend the Spectator, the silent gentleman, with a tobacco-stopper made by Will Wimble, telling him that Will had been busy all the early part of the winter in turning great quantities of them, and had made a present of one to every gentleman in the county who had good principles and smoked. When Sir Roger was driving in a hackney-coach he called upon the coachman to stop, and when the man came to the window asked him if he smoked. While Sir Roger's companion was wondering "what this would end in," the knight bid his Jehu to "stop by the way at any good Tobacconist's, and take in a Roll of their best Virginia." And when he visited Squire's near Gray's Inn Gate, his first act was to call for a clean pipe, a paper of tobacco, a dish of coffee, a newspaper and a wax candle; and all the boys in the coffee-room ran to serve him. The wax candle was of course a convenience in matchless days for pipe-lighting. The "paper of tobacco" was the equivalent of what is now vulgarly called a "screw" of tobacco.

The practice of selling tobacco in small paper packets was common, and moralists naturally had something to say about the fate of an author's work, when the leaves of his books found their ultimate use as wrappers for the weed. "For as no mortal author," says Addison, "in the ordinary fate and vicissitude of things, knows to what use his works may, some time or other, be applied, a man may often meet with very celebrated names in a paper of tobacco. I have lighted my pipe more than once with the writings of a prelate."

Addison and Steele smoked, and so did Prior, who seems to have had a weakness at times for low company. After spending an evening with Oxford, Bolingbroke, Pope and Swift, it is recorded that he would go "and smoke a pipe, and drink a bottle of ale, with a common soldier and his wife, in Long Acre, before he went to bed." Some of Prior's poems, as Thackeray caustically remarks, smack not a little of the conversation of his Long Acre friends. Pope for awhile attended the symposium at Button's coffee-house, where Addison was the centre of the coterie--he describes himself as sitting with them till two in the morning over punch and Burgundy amid the fumes of tobacco--but such a way of life did not suit his sickly constitution, and he soon withdrew. It is not likely that he smoked.

The attractions and the atmosphere of provincial coffee-houses were much the same as those of the London resorts. A German gentleman who visited Cambridge in July and August 1710 remarked that in the Greeks' coffee-house in that town, in the morning and after 3 o'clock in the afternoon, you could meet the chief professors and doctors, who read the papers over a cup of coffee and a pipe of tobacco. One of the learned doctors took the German visitor to the weekly meeting of a Music Club in one of the colleges. Here were assembled bachelors, masters and doctors of music of the University--no professionals were employed--who performed vocal and instrumental music to their mutual gratification, though, apparently, not to the satisfaction of the visitor, who records his opinion that the music was "very poor." "It lasted," he says, "till 11 P.M., there was besides smoking and drinking of wine, though we did not do much of either. At 11 the reckoning was called for, and each person paid 2s."

There was clearly no prejudice against smoking at Cambridge. Abraham de la Pryme notes in his diary for the year 1694 that when it was rumoured in May of that year that a certain house opposite one of the colleges was haunted, strange noises being heard in it, several scholars of the college said, "Come, fetch us a good pitcher of ale, and tobacco and pipes, and wee'l sit up and see this spirit." The ale was duly provided, the pipes were lit, and the courageous smokers spent the night in the house, sitting "singing and drinking there till morning," but, alas! they neither saw nor heard anything.

Smoking was still popular also at Oxford. A. D'Anvers, in her "Academia; or the Humours of Oxford," 1691, speaks, indeed, of undergraduates who, when they could not get tobacco, did much as the parson of Thornton is reputed to have done, as already related in Chapter II, i.e. they condescended to smoke fragments of mats. With this may be compared the macaronic lines:

At si   *Mundungus* desit: tum non *funcare* recusant **Brown-Paper** tosta, vel quod fit arundine bed-mat.

Tobacco, in Queen Anne's time, still maintained its hold over large classes of the people, and was still dominant in most places of public resort; but there were signs of change in various directions as we have seen, and smoking had to a large extent ceased to be fashionable. Pepys has very few allusions to tobacco; Evelyn fewer still. There is little evidence as to whether or not the gallants of the Restoration Court smoked; but considering the foppery of their attire and manners, it seems almost certain that tobacco was not in favour among them. The beaux with their full wigs--they carried combs of ivory or tortoiseshell in their pockets with which they publicly combed their flowing locks--their dandy canes and scented, laced handkerchiefs, were not the men to enjoy the flavour of tobacco in a pipe. They were still tobacco-worshippers; but they did not smoke. The Indian weed retained its empire over the men (and women) of fashion by changing its form. The beaux were the devotees of snuff. The deftly handled pinch pleasantly titillated their nerves, and the dexterous use of the snuff-box, moreover, could also serve the purposes of vanity by displaying the beautiful whiteness of the hand, and the splendour of the rings upon the fingers. The curled darlings of the late seventeenth century and the "pretty fellows" of Queen Anne's time did not forswear tobacco, but they abjured smoking. Snuff-taking was universal in the fashionable world among both men and women; and the development of this habit made smoking unfashionable.

VII
SMOKING UNFASHIONABLE:
EARLY GEORGIAN DAYS

Lord Fopling smokes not--for his teeth afraid;
Sir Tawdry smokes not--for he wears brocade.
ISAAC HAWKINS BROWNE, circa 1740.

With the reign of Queen Anne tobacco had entered on a period, destined to be of long duration, when smoking was to a very large extent under a social ban. Pipe-smoking was unfashionable--that is to say, was not practised by men of fashion, and was for the most part regarded as "low" or provincial--from the time named until well into the reign of Queen Victoria. The social taboo was by no means universal--some of the exceptions will be noted in these pages--but speaking broadly, the general, almost universal smoking of tobacco which had been characteristic of the earlier decades of the seventeenth century did not again prevail until within living memory.

Throughout the eighteenth century the use of tobacco for smoking was largely confined to the middle and humbler classes of society. To smoke was characteristic of the "cit," of the country squire, of the clergy (especially of the country parsons), and of those of lower social status. But at the same time it must be borne in mind that then, as since, the dictates of fashion and the conventions of society were little regarded by many artists and men of letters.

In the preceding chapter I quoted from Addison's diary of a retired tradesman in the Spectator *of 1712. The periodical publications of a generation or so later paid the great essayist the flattery of imitation in this respect as in others. In the* Connoisseur of George Colman and Bonnell Thornton, for instance, there is, in 1754, the description of a citizen's Sunday. The good man, having sent his family to church in the morning, goes off himself to Mother Redcap's, a favourite tavern-- suburban in those days--or house of call for City tradesmen. There he smokes half a pipe and drinks a pint of ale. In the evening at another tavern he smokes a pipe and drinks two pints of cider, winding up the inane day at his club, where he smokes three pipes before coming home at twelve to go to bed and sleep soundly.

The week-end habit was strong among London tradesmen in those days. An-other Connoisseur paper of 1754 refers to the citizens' country-boxes as dusty re-treats, because they were always built in close contiguity to the highway so that the inhabitants could watch the traffic, in the absence of anything more sensible to do, where "the want of London smoke is supplied by the smoke of Virginia tobacco," and where "our chief citizens are accustomed to pass the end and the beginning of every week." In the following year there is a description of a visit to Vauxhall by a worthy citizen with his wife and two daughters. After supper the poor man sadly laments that he cannot have his pipe, because his wife, with social ambitions, deems that it is "ungenteel to smoke, where any ladies are in company."

Again, in the Connoisseur's *rival, the* World, founded and conducted by Ed-ward Moore, there is a letter, in the number dated February 19, 1756, from a citizen who says: "I have the honour to be a member of a certain club in this city, where it is a standing order, That the paper called the World be constantly brought upon the table, with clean glasses, pipes and tobacco, every Thursday after dinner."

The country gentlemen of the time followed the hounds and enjoyed rural sports of all kinds, drank ale, and smoked tobacco. They had their smoking-rooms too. Walter Gale, schoolmaster at Mayfield, Sussex, noted in his Journal under date March 26, 1751: "I went to Mr. Baker's for the list of scholars, and found him alone in the smoaking-room; he ordered a pint of mild beer for me, an extraordinary thing." Gale himself was a regular smoker, and too fond of pints of ale.

Fielding has immortalized the squire of the mid-eighteenth century in his pic-ture of that sporting, roaring, swearing, drinking, smoking, affectionate, irascible, blundering, altogether extraordinary owner of broad acres, Squire Western. We may shrewdly suspect that the portrait of Western is somewhat over-coloured, and cannot fairly be taken as typical; but there is sufficient evidence to show that in some respects at least--in his enthusiasm for sport and love of ale and tobacco--Western is representative of the country squires of his day.

In a World *of 1755 there is a description of a noisy, hearty, drinking, devil-may-care country gentleman, in which it is said, "he makes no scruple to take his pipe and pot at an alehouse with the very dregs of the people." In a* Connoisseur of 1754 a fine gentleman from London, making a visit in a country-house, is taking his breakfast with the ladies in the afternoon, when they had their tea, for, says he, "I should infallibly have perished, had I staied in the hall, amidst the jargon of toasts and the fumes of tobacco." When Horace Walpole was staying with his father at his Norfolk country-seat, Houghton, in September 1737, Gray wrote to him from Cambridge: "You are in a confusion of wine, and roaring, and hunting, and tobacco, and, heaven be praised, you too can pretty well bear it." But Gray had no objection to tobacco. He lived at Cambridge, and the dons and residents there (as at Oxford), not to speak of the undergraduates, were as partial to their pipes as the men who went out from among them to become country parsons, and to share the country squire's liking for tobacco. Gray wrote to Warton from Cambridge in April 1749 saying: "Time will settle my conscience, time will reconcile me to this languid companion (ennui); we shall smoke, we shall tipple, we shall doze together"--a striking picture of University life in the sleepy days of the eighteenth century. Gray's testimony by no means stands alone. In November 1730 Roger North wrote to his son Montague, then an undergraduate at Cambridge, saying: "I would be loath you should confirm the scandal charged upon the universities of learning chiefly to smoke and to drink."

At Oxford in early Georgian days a profound calm--so far as study was concerned--appears to have prevailed. Little work was done, but much tobacco was smoked. In 1733 a satire was published, violently attacking the Fellows of various colleges. According to this satirist the occupation of the Magdalen Fellow was to

drink, look big,
Smoke much, think little, curse the freeborn Whig--

from which it may not unreasonably be surmised that the author was a Tory; and however little enthusiasm there may have been at Oxford in those days for learning and study, there was plenty of life in political animosities.

Another witness to the dons' love of tobacco is Thomas Warton. In his "Progress of Discontent," written in 1746, he plaintively sang:

Return, ye days when endless pleasure
I found in reading or in leisure!
When calm around the Common Room
I puff'd my daily pipe's perfume!
Rode for a stomach, and inspected,
At annual bottlings, corks selected:
And dined untax'd, untroubled, under
The portrait of our pious Founder!

Warton and another Oxford smoker of some distinction--the Rev. William Crowe, who was Public Orator from 1784 to 1829--are both said to have been, like Prior, rather fond of frequenting the company of persons of humble rank and little education, with whom they would drink their ale and smoke their pipes.

Mr. A.D. Godley, in his "Oxford in the Eighteenth Century," gives an excellent English version of the Latin original of one of the Christ Church "Carmina Quadragesmalia," which affords much the same picture of the daily life of an Oxford Fellow in the days when George I was king. This good man lives strictly by rule, and each returning day--

Ne'er swerves a hairbreadth from the same old way.
Always within the memory of men
He's risen at eight and gone to bed at ten:
The same old cat his College room partakes,

The same old scout his bed each morning makes:
On mutton roast he daily dines in state
(Whole flocks have perished to supply his plate),
Takes just one turn to catch the westering sun,
Then reads the paper, as he's always done;
Soon cracks in Common-room the same old jokes,

Drinking three glasses ere three pipes he smokes:--
And what he did while Charles our throne did fill
'Neath George's heir you'll find him doing still.

It seems to have been taken for granted that country parsons smoked. Smoking was universal among their male parishioners from the squire to the labourer (when he could afford it), so that it was only natural that the parson, with little to do, and in those days not too much inclination to do it, should be as fond of his pipe as the rest of the world around him. In a World of 1756 there is an account of a country gentleman entertaining one evening the vicar of the parish, and the host as a matter of course proceeds to order a bottle of wine with pipes and tobacco to be placed on the table. The vicar forthwith "filled his pipe, and drank very cordially to my friend," his host. One cannot doubt that Laurence Sterne, that most remarkable of country parsons, smoked. His "My Uncle Toby" is among the immortals, and Toby without his pipe is unimaginable.

The most famous of country clergymen of the early Georgian period is, of course, Fielding's lovable and immortal Parson Adams. Throughout "Joseph Andrews" the parson smokes at every opportunity. At his first appearance on the scene, in the inn kitchen, he calls for a pipe of tobacco before taking his place at the fireside. The next morning, when he fails to obtain a desired loan from the landlord, Adams, extremely dejected at his disappointment, immediately applies to his pipe, "his constant friend and comfort in his affliction," and leans over the rails of the gallery overlooking the inn-yard, devoting himself to meditation, "assisted by the inspiring fumes of tobacco." Later on, in the parlour of the country Justice of the Peace, who condemned his prisoners before he had taken the depositions of the witnesses against them, and who, by the way, also lit his pipe while his clerk performed this necessary duty, Adams, when his character has been cleared, sits down with the company and takes a cheerful glass and applies himself vigorously to smoking. A few hours later, when the parson, Fanny, and their guide are driven by a storm of rain to take shelter in a wayside ale-house, Adams "immediately procured himself a good fire, a toast and ale, and a pipe, and began to smoke with great content, utterly forgetting everything that had happened." In the same inn, after Mrs. Slipslop has appeared and disappeared, Adams smokes three pipes and takes "a comfortable nap in a great chair," so leaving the lovers, Joseph and Fanny, to enjoy a delightful time together.

At another inn a country squire is discovered smoking his pipe by the door and the parson promptly joins him. Again, he smokes before he goes to bed, and before he breakfasts the next morning; and when he goes into the inn garden with the host who is willing to trust him, both host and parson light their pipes before beginning to gossip. Farther on, when the hospitable Mr. Wilson takes the weary wayfarers in, Parson Adams loses no time in filling himself with ale, as Fielding puts it, and lighting his pipe. The menfolk--Wilson, Adams and Joseph--have to spend the night seated round the fire, but apparently Adams is the only one who seeks the solace of tobacco. It is significant that Wilson, in telling the story of his dissipated early life, classes smoking with "singing, holloaing, wrangling, drinking, toasting," and other diversions of "jolly companions."

There is no mention of Parson Trulliber's pipe, but that pig-breeder and lover can hardly have been a non-smoker. Both the other clerical characters who appear in the book, the Roman Catholic priest who makes an equivocal appearance in the eighth chapter of the third book, and Parson Barnabas, who thinks that his own sermons are at least equal to Tillotson's, smoke their pipes. The other smokers in "Joseph Andrews" are the surgeon and the exciseman who, early in the story, are found sitting in the inn kitchen with Parson Barnabas, "smoking their pipes over some syderand"--the mysterious "cup" being a mixture of cider and something spirituous--and Joseph's father, old Gaffer Andrews, who appears at the end of the story, and complains bitterly that he wants his pipe, not having had a whiff that morning.

Fielding himself smoked his pipe. When his play "The Wedding Day" was produced by Garrick in 1743, various suggestions were made to the author as to the excision of certain passages, and the modification of one of the scenes. Garrick pressed for certain omissions, but--"No, damn them," said Fielding, "if the scene is not a good one, let them find that out"; and then, according to Murphy, he retired to the green-room, where, during the progress of the play, he smoked his pipe and drank champagne. Presently he heard the sound of hissing, and when Garrick came in and explained that the audience had hissed the scene he had wished to have modified, all Fielding said was: "Oh, damn them, they have found it out, have they!"

Simon Fraser, Lord Lovat, the crafty old Jacobite who took part in the rising of 1745 and who was executed on Tower Hill in 1747, was a smoker. The pipe which he was reported to have smoked on the evening before his execution, together with his snuff-box and a canvas tobacco-bag, were for many years in the possession of the Society of Cogers, the famous debating society of Fleet Street.

It has sometimes been said that Swift smoked; but this is a mistake. He had a fancy for taking tobacco in a slightly different way from the fashionable mode of taking snuff. He told Stella that he had left off snuff altogether, and then in the very next sentence remarked that he had "a noble roll of tobacco for grating, very good." And in a later letter to Stella, May 24, 1711, he asked if she still snuffed, and went on to say, in sentences that seem to contradict one another: "I have left it off, and when anybody offers me their box, I take about a tenth part of what I used to do, then just smell to it, and privately fling the rest away. I keep to my tobacco still, as you say; but even much less of that than formerly, only mornings and evenings, and very seldom in the day." One might infer from this that he smoked, but this Swift never did. His practice was to snuff up cut and dried tobacco, which was sometimes just coloured with Spanish snuff. This he did all his life, but as the mixture he took was not technically snuff, he never owned that he took snuff.

Another cleric of the period, well known to fame, who took snuff but also loved his pipe, was Samuel Wesley, rector of Epworth, Lincolnshire, from 1697 to 1735. He not only smoked his pipe, but sang its praises:

> In these raw mornings, when I'm freezing ripe,
> What can compare with a tobacco-pipe?
> Primed, cocked and toucht, 'twould better heat a man
> Than ten Bath Faggots or Scotch warming-pan.

Samuel's greater son, John Wesley, did not share the parental love of a pipe. He spoke of the use of tobacco as "an uncleanly and unwholesome self-indulgence," and described snuffing as "a silly, nasty, dirty custom."

The London clergy seem to have smoked at one time as a matter of course at their gatherings at Sion College, their headquarters. An entry in the records under date February 14, 1682, relating to a Court Meeting, runs: "Paid Maddocks [the

Messenger] for Attendinge and Pipes 6d." How long pipes continued to be concomitants of the meetings of the College's General Court I cannot say; but smoking and the annual dinners were long associated. At the anniversary feast in 1743 there were two tables to provide for, the total number of guests being about thirty, and two "corses" to each. The cost of the food, as Canon Pearce tells us in his excellent and entertaining book on the College and its Library, was L19 15s., or rather more than 13s. a head. The bill for wines and tobacco amounted to five guineas, or about 3s. 6d. a head, and for this modest sum the thirty convives enjoyed eleven gallons of "Red Oporto," one of "White Lisbon," and three of "Mountain," to the accompaniment of two pounds of tobacco (at 3s. 4d. the pound) smoked in "half a groce of pipes" (at 1s.).

The examples and illustrations which have been given so far in this chapter relate to tradesmen and merchants, country gentlemen and the clergy. Other professional men smoked--we read in Fielding's "Amelia" of a doctor who in the evening "smoked his pillow-pipe, as the phrase is"--and among the rest of the people of equal or lower social standing smoking was as generally practised as in the preceding century. Handel, I may note, enjoyed his pipe. Dr. Burney, when a schoolboy at Chester, was "extremely curious to see so extraordinary a man," so when Handel went through that city in 1741 on his way to Ireland, young Burney "watched him narrowly as long as he remained in Chester," and among other things, had the felicity of seeing the great man "smoke a pipe, over a dish of coffee, at the Exchange Coffee-house," which was under the old Town Hall that stood opposite the present King's School, and in front of the present Town Hall.

Gonzales, in his "Voyage to Great Britain," 1731, says that the use of tobacco was "very universal, and indeed not improper for so moist a climate." He tells us that though the taverns were very numerous yet the ale-houses were much more so. These ale-houses were visited by the inferior tradesmen, mechanics, journeymen, porters, coachmen, carmen, servants, and others whose pockets were not equal to the price of a glass of wine, which, apparently, was the more usual thing to call for at a tavern, properly so called. In the ale-house men of the various classes and occupations enumerated, says the traveller, would "sit promiscuously in common dirty rooms, with large fires, and clouds of tobacco, where one that is not used to them can scarce breathe or see."

The antiquary Hearne has left on record an account of a curious smoking match held at Oxford in 1723. It began at two o'clock in the afternoon of September 4 on a scaffold specially erected for the purpose "over against the Theatre in Oxford ... just at Finmore's, an alehouse." The conditions were that any one (man or woman) who could smoke out three ounces of tobacco first, without drinking or going off the stage, should have 12s. "Many tryed," continues Hearne, "and 'twas thought that a journeyman taylour of St. Peter's in the East would have been victor, he smoking faster than, and being many pipes before, the rest: but at last he was so sick, that 'twas thought he would have dyed; and an old man, that had been a souldier, and smoaked gently, came off conqueror, smoaking the three ounces quite out, and he told one (from whom I had it) that, after it, he smoaked 4 or 5 pipes the same evening." The old soldier was a well-seasoned veteran.

Another foreign visitor to England, the Abbe Le Blanc, who was over here about 1730, found English customs rather trying. "Even at table," he says, "where they serve desserts, they do but show them, and presently take away everything, even to the tablecloth. By this the English, whom politeness does not permit to tell the ladies their company is troublesome, give them notice to retire.... The table is immediately covered with mugs, bottles and glasses; and often with pipes of tobacco. All things thus disposed, the ceremony of toasts begins."

The frowns and remonstrances of Quarterly and Monthly Meetings of Friends had not succeeded in putting the Quakers' pipes out. In a list of sea stores put on board a vessel called by the un-Quaker-like name of The Charming Polly, which brought a party of Friends across the Atlantic from Philadelphia in 1756, we find "In Samuel Fothergill's new chest ... Tobacco ... a Hamper ... a Barrel ... a box of pipes." The provident Samuel was well found for a long voyage.

The non-smokers were the men of fashion and those who followed them in preferring the snuff-box to the pipe. Sometimes, apparently, they chewed. A World of 1754 pokes fun at the "pretty" young men who "take pains to appear manly. But alas! the methods they pursue, like most mistaken applications, rather aggravate the calamity. Their drinking and raking only makes them look like old maids. Their swearing is almost as shocking as it would be in the other sex. Their chewing tobacco not only offends, but makes us apprehensive at the same time that the poor things will be sick," as they certainly well deserved to be. To chew might be "manly," but it will be observed that smoking is not mentioned. No reputation for manliness could be achieved by even the affectation of a pipe. Similarly, in Bramston's "Man of Taste," various fashionable tastes are described, but there is no mention of tobacco.

In Townley's well-known two-act farce "High Life Below Stairs," 1759, the servants take their masters' and mistresses' titles and ape their ways. The menservants--the Dukes and Sir Harrys--offer one another snuff. "Taste this snuff, Sir Harry," says the "Duke." "'Tis good rappee," replies "Sir Harry." "Right Strasburgh, I assure you, and of my own importing," says the knowing ducal valet. "The city people adulterate it so confoundedly," he continues, "that I always import my own snuff;" and in similar vein he goes on in imitation of his master, the genuine Duke. These servants copy the talk and style (with a difference) of their employers; but smoking is never mentioned. The real Dukes and Sir Harrys took snuff with a grace, but they did not do anything so low as to smoke, and their menservants faithfully aped their preferences and their aversions.

Negative evidence of this kind is abundant; and positive statements of the aversion of the beaux from smoking are not lacking. Dodsley's "Collection" contains a satirical poem called "A Pipe of Tobacco," which was written in imitation of six different poets. The author was Isaac Hawkins Browne, and the poets imitated were the Laureate Cibber, Philips, Thomson, Young, Pope, and Swift. The first imitation is called "A New Year's Ode," and contains three recitatives, three airs and a chorus. One of the airs will suffice as a sample:

> Happy mortal! he who knows
> Pleasure which a Pipe bestows;
> Curling eddies climb the room
> Wafting round a mild perfume.

Number two, which was intended as a burlesque of Philips's "Splendid Shilling," is really pretty and must be given entire. It reveals unsuspected beauties in the simple "churchwarden," or "yard of clay":

> Little tube of mighty pow'r,

Charmer of an idle hour,
Object of my warm desire,
Lip of wax, and eye of fire:
And thy snowy taper waist,
With my finger gently brac'd;
And thy pretty swelling crest,
With my little stopper prest,
And the sweetest bliss of blisses,
Breathing from thy balmy kisses.
Happy thrice, and thrice agen,
Happiest he of happy men;
Who when agen the night returns,
When agen the taper burns;
When agen the cricket's gay,
(Little cricket, full of play)
Can afford his tube to feed
With the fragrant Indian weed:
Pleasure for a nose divine,
Incense of the god of wine.
Happy thrice, and thrice agen,
Happiest he of happy men.

Imitations three and five praise the leaf in less happy strains, though number five has a line worth noting for our purpose, in which tobacco is spoken of as

By ladies hated, hated by the beaux.

The sixth sinks to ribaldry. Number four contains evidence of the distaste for smoking among the beaux in the lines:

Coxcombs prefer the tickling sting of snuff;
Yet all their claim to wisdom is--a puff;
Lord Foplin smokes not--for his teeth afraid:
Sir Tawdry smokes not--for he wears brocade.

Ladies, when pipes are brought, affect to swoon;
They love no smoke, except the smoke of Town;
But courtiers hate the puffing tube--no matter,
Strange if they love the breath that cannot flatter!

*   *   *   *   *   *   *   *

Yet crowds remain, who still its worth proclaim,
While some for pleasure smoke, and some for Fame.

The satirist wrote truly that after all the fashionable abstainers had been de-
ducted, crowds remained, who smoked as heartily as their predecessors of a century
earlier. The populace was still on the side of tobacco. This was well shown in 1732
when Sir Robert Walpole proposed special excise duties on tobacco, and brought a
Bill into Parliament which would have given his excisemen powers of inquisition
which were much resented by the people generally. The controversy produced a
host of squibs and caricatures, most of which were directed against the measure.
The Bill was defeated in 1733, and great and general were the rejoicings. When the
news reached Derby on April 19 in that year, the dealers in tobacco caused all the
bells in the Derby churches to be rung, and we may be sure that this rather unusual
performance was highly popular. The withdrawal of the odious duty was further
celebrated by caricatures and "poetical" chants of triumph. One of the leading opponents of the Bill had been a well-known puffing tobacconist named Bradley, who
was accustomed to describe his wares as "the best in Christendom"; and when the
Bill was defeated Bradley's portrait was published for popular circulation, above
these lines:

Behold the man, who, when a gloomy band
Of vile excisemen threatened all the land,
Help'd to deliver from their harpy gripe
The cheerful bottle and the social pipe.
O rare Ben Bradley! may for this the bowl,
Still **unexcised,** rejoice thy honest soul!
May still **the best in Christendom** for this
Cleave to thy stopper, and compleat thy bliss!

This print is now chiefly of interest because the plate was adorned with a tiny etching by Hogarth, in which appear the figures of the British Lion and Britannia, both with pipes in their mouths, Britannia being seated on a cask of tobacco.

Hogarth was fond of introducing the pipe into his plates. In the tail-piece to his works, which he prepared a few months before his death, and which he called The Bathos, or Manner of Sinking in Sublime Paintings, the end of everything is represented. Time himself, supported against a broken column, is expiring, his scythe falling from his grasp and a long clay pipe breaking in two as it falls from his lips. This was issued in 1764--Hogarth's last published work. In the plate which shows the execution of Thomas Idle, in the "Industry and Idleness" series, Hogarth depicts the little hangman smoking a short pipe as he sits on the top of the gallows, waiting for his victim. The familiar plate of A Modern Midnight Conversation shows a parson in surplice and wig smoking like a furnace while he ladles punch from a bowl--probably meant for a portrait of the notorious Orator Henley. Most of the other guests are also shown smoking long clay pipes.

Hogarth's subscription ticket for the print of Sigismunda *was* Time Smoking a Picture (1761). It represents an old man sitting on a fragment of statuary and smoking a long pipe against a picture of a landscape which stands upon an easel before him. Below, on his left, is a large jar labelled "Varnish." The figure of Time is nude and has large wings. Volumes of smoke are pouring against the surface of the picture from both his mouth and the bowl of his long clay pipe. In The Stage-Coach, or Country Inn-yard, is shown an old woman smoking a pipe in the "basket" of the coach. The plate of The Distrest Poet (1736) shows four books and three tobacco-pipes on a shelf. In the second of the "Election" series--the Canvassing for Votes (1755)--a barber and a cobbler, seated at the table in the right-hand corner, are both smoking long pipes. Apparently they are discussing the taking of Portobello by Admiral Vernon in 1739 with only six ships; for the barber is illustrating his talk by pointing with his twisted pipe-stem to six fragments which he has broken from the stem and arranged on the table in the shape of a crescent. In the frontispiece which Hogarth drew in 1762 for Garrick's farce of "The Farmer's Return from London," the worthy farmer, seated in his great chair, holds out a large mug in one hand to be filled with ale, while the other supports his long pipe, which he is smoking with evident enjoyment.

Hogarth himself was a confirmed pipe-lover. When he and Thornhill and their three companions set out from Gravesend for the final stage, up the river, of their famous "Five Days Peregrination," we are told that they hired a boat with clean straw, and laid in a bottle of wine, pipes, tobacco, and light, and so came merrily up the river. The arm-chair in which Hogarth was wont to sit and smoke is still preserved in his house at Chiswick, which has been bought and preserved as a memorial of the moralist-painter; and in the garden of the house may still be seen the remains of the mulberry tree under which Mr. Austin Dobson suggests that Hogarth and Fielding may have sat and smoked their pipes together in the days when George was King.

VIII
SMOKING UNFASHIONABLE (continued): LATER GEORGIAN DAYS

Says the Pipe to the Snuff-box, I can't understand
What the ladies and gentlemen see in your face,
That you are in fashion all over the land,
And I am so much fallen into disgrace.
WILLIAM COWPER.
(From a letter to the Rev. John Newton, May 28, 1782.)

Smoking has gone out," said Johnson in talk at St. Andrews, one day in 1773. "To be sure," he continued, "it is a shocking thing, blowing smoke out of our mouths into other people's mouths, eyes and noses, and having the same thing done to us; yet I cannot account why a thing which requires so little exertion, and yet preserves the mind from total vacuity, should have gone out." Johnson did not trouble himself to think of how much the vagaries of fashion account for stranger vicissitudes in manners and customs than the rise and fall of the smoking-habit; nor did he probably foresee how slowly but surely the taste for smoking, even in the circles most influenced by fashion, would revive. Boswell tells us that although the sage himself never smoked, yet he had a high opinion of the practice as a sedative influence; and Hawkins heard him say on one occasion that insanity had grown more frequent since smoking had gone out of fashion, which shows that even Johnson could fall a victim to the post hoc propter hoc fallacy.

More than one writer of recent days has absurdly misrepresented Johnson as a smoker. The author of a book on tobacco published a few years ago wrote-- "Dr. Johnson smoked like a furnace"--a grotesquely untrue statement--and "all his

friends, Goldsmith, Reynolds, Garrick, were his companions in tobacco-worship."
Reynolds, we know--

> When they talk'd of their Raphaels, Corregios, and stuff,
> He shifted his trumpet, and only took snuff.

Johnson and all his company took snuff, as every one in the fashionable world,
and a great many others outside that charmed circle, did; but Johnson did not smoke,
and I doubt whether any of the others did.

There is ample evidence, apart from Johnson's dictum, that in the latter part
of the eighteenth century smoking had "gone out." In Mrs. Climenson's "Passages
from the Diaries of Mrs. Lybbe Powys," we hear of a bundle of papers at Hardwick
House, near Whitchurch, Oxon, which bears the unvarnished title "Dick's Debts."
This Dick was a Captain Richard Powys who had a commission in the Guards, and
died at the early age of twenty-six in the year 1768. This list of debts, it appears, gives
"the most complete catalogue of the expenses of a dandy of the Court of George II,
consisting chiefly of swords, buckles, lace, Valenciennes and point d'Espagne, gold
and amber-headed canes, tavern bills and chair hire." But in all the ample detail of
Captain Powys's list of extravagances there is nothing directly or indirectly relating
to smoking. The beaux of the time did not smoke.

In the whole sixteen volumes of Walpole's correspondence, as so admirably
edited by Mrs. Toynbee, there is scarcely a mention of tobacco; and the same may
be said of other collections of letters of the same period--the Selwyn letters, the
Delany correspondence, and so on. Neither Walpole nor any member of the world
in which he lived would appear to have smoked. In Miss Burney's "Evelina," 1778,
from the beginning to the end of the book there is no mention whatever of tobacco
or of smoking. Apparently the vulgar Branghtons were not vulgar enough to smoke.
Such use of tobacco was considered low, and was confined to the classes of society
indicated in the preceding chapter. One of the characters in Macklin's "Love a la
Mode," 1760, is described as "dull, dull as an alderman, after six pounds of turtle,
four bottles of port, and twelve pipes of tobacco."

A satirical print by Rowlandson contains A Man of Fashion's Journal, dated
May 1, 1802. The "man of fashion" rides and drinks, goes to the play, gambles and

bets, but his journal contains no reference to smoking. Rowlandson himself smoked, and so did his brother caricaturist, Gillray. Angelo says that they would sometimes meet at such resorts of the "low" as the Bell, the Coal Hole, or the Coach and Horses, and would enter into the common chat of the room, smoke and drink together, and then "sometimes early, sometimes late, shake hands at the door--look up at the stars, say it is a pretty night, and depart, one for the Adelphi, the other to St. James's Street, each to his bachelor's bed."

But outside the fashionable world pipes were still in full blast, and in many places of resort the atmosphere was as beclouded with tobacco-smoke as in earlier days. Grosley, in his "Tour to London," 1765, says that there were regular clubs, which were held in coffee-houses and taverns at fixed days and hours, when wine, beer, tea, pipes and tobacco helped to amuse the company.

Angelo gives some lively pictures of scenes of this kind in the London of about 1780. The Turk's Head, in Gerrard Street, was the meeting-place for "a knot of worthies, principally 'Sons of St. Luke,' or the children of Thespis, and mostly votaries of Bacchus," as the old fencing-master, who loved a little "fine writing," describes them; and here they sat, he says, "taking their punch and smoking, the prevailing custom of the time." About the same time (circa 1790) an evening resort for purposes mostly vicious was the famous Dog and Duck, in St. George's Fields. "The long room," says Angelo, "if I may depend on my memory, was on the ground floor, and all the benches were filled with motley groups, eating, drinking, and smoking." Angelo also mentions the "Picnic Society," a celebrated resort of fashion at the beginning of the nineteenth century, where the odour of tobacco never penetrated. It afforded, he says in his fine way, "a sort of antipodeal contrast to these smoking tavern clubs of the old city of Trinobantes." The same writer speaks of a certain Monsieur Liviez whom he met in Paris in 1772, who had been one of the first dancers at the Italian Opera House, and maitre de ballet *at Drury Lane Theatre. This gentleman was addicted to self-indulgence, loved good eating, and good and ample drinking, and moreover kept "late hours,* a l'Anglaise, smoked his pipe, and drank oceans of punch."

Coleridge, in the "Biographia Literaria," gives an amusing account of his own experience of an attempt to smoke in company with a party of tradesmen. In 1795 he was travelling about the country endeavouring to secure subscriptions to the periodical publication he had started called The Watchman. At Birmingham one day he dined with a worthy tradesman, who, after dinner, importuned him "to smoke a pipe with him, and two or three other illuminati of the same rank." The remainder of the moving story must be told in Coleridge's own words. "I objected," he says, "both because I was engaged to spend the evening with a minister and his friends, and because I had never smoked except once or twice in my life-time, and then it was herb tobacco mixed with Oronooko. On the assurance, however, that the tobacco was equally mild, and seeing too that it was of a yellow colour,--not forgetting the lamentable difficulty I have always experienced in saying, 'No,' and in abstaining from what the people about me were doing,--I took half a pipe, filling the lower half of the bole with salt. I was soon, however, compelled to resign it, in consequence of a giddiness and distressful feeling in my eyes, which, as I had drunk but a single glass of ale, must, I knew, have been the effect of the tobacco. Soon after, deeming myself recovered, I sallied forth to my engagement; but the walk and the fresh air brought on all the symptoms again, and I had scarcely entered the minister's drawing-room, and opened a small pacquet of letters, which he had received from Bristol for me, ere I sank back on the sofa in a sort of swoon rather than sleep. Fortunately I had found just time enough to inform him of the confused state of my feelings, and of the occasion. For here and thus I lay, my face like a wall that is white-washing, deathly pale, and with the cold drops of perspiration running down it from my forehead, while one after another there dropped in the different gentlemen, who had been invited to meet, and spend the evening with me, to the number of from fifteen to twenty. As the poison of tobacco acts but for a short time, I at length awoke from insensibility, and looked round on the party, my eyes dazzled by the candles which had been lighted in the interim. By way of relieving my embarrassment one of the gentlemen began the conversation with 'Have you seen a paper to-day, Mr. Coleridge?' 'Sir,' I replied, rubbing my eyes, 'I am far from convinced that a Christian is permitted to read either newspapers or any other works of merely political and temporary interest.' This remark, so ludicrously inapposite to, or rather, incongruous with, the purpose for which I was known to have visited Birmingham, and to assist me in which they were all met, produced an involuntary and general burst of laughter; and seldom indeed have I passed so many delightful hours as I enjoyed in that room from the moment of that laugh till an early hour the next morning."

All's well that ends well; but one cannot help wondering what kind of tobacco it was that the Birmingham tradesman used, a half pipeful of which had such a deadly effect--but perhaps the effect was due to the salt, not to the tobacco.

In the year after that which witnessed Coleridge's adventure, i.e. in 1796, a tobacco-box with a history was the subject of a legal decision. This box, made of common horn and small enough to be carried in the pocket, was bought for four-pence by an overseer of the poor in the time of Queen Anne, and was presented by him in 1713 to the Society of Past Overseers of the parish of St. Margaret, Westminster. In 1720 the Society, in memory of the donor, ornamented the lid with a silver rim; and at intervals thereafter additions were made to an extraordinary extent to the box and its casings. Hogarth engraved within the lid in 1746 a bust of the victor of Culloden. Gradually the horn box was enshrined within one case after another--usually silver lined with velvet--each case bearing inscribed plates commemorating persons or events. A Past Overseer who detained the box in 1793 had to give it back after three years of litigation. A case of octagon shape records the triumph of Justice, and Lord Chancellor Loughborough pronouncing his decree for the restitution of the box on March 5, 1796. In later days many and various additions have been made to the many coverings of the box, recording public events of interest.

Notwithstanding the unfashionableness of tobacco, there were still some noteworthy smokers to be found among the clergy. Dr. Sumner, head master of Harrow, who died in 1771, was devoted to his pipe. The greatest of clerical "tobacconists" of late eighteenth century and early nineteenth century date was the once famous Dr. Parr. It was from him that Dr. Sumner learned to smoke. When he and Parr got together Sumner was in the habit of refilling his pipe again and again in such a way as to be unobserved, at the same time begging Parr not to depart till he had finished his pipe, in order that he might detain him, we are told, in the evening as long as possible.

Parr was not a model smoker. He was brutally overbearing towards other folk, and would accept no invitation except on the understanding that he might smoke when and where he liked. It was his invariable practice, wherever he might be visiting, to smoke a pipe as soon as he had got out of bed. His biographer says--"The ladies were obliged to bear his tobacco, or to give up his company; and at Hatton

(1786-1825) now and then he was the tyrant of the fireside." Parr was capable of smoking twenty pipes in an evening, and described himself as "rolling volcanic fumes of tobacco to the ceiling" while he worked at his desk. At a dinner which was given at Trinity College, Cambridge, to the Duke of Gloucester, as Chancellor of the University, when the cloth was removed, Parr at once started his pipe and began, says one who was present, "blowing a cloud into the faces of his neighbours, much to their annoyance, and causing royalty to sneeze by the stimulating stench of mundungus." It is surprising that people were willing to put up with such bad manners as Parr was accustomed to exhibit; but his reputation was then great, and he traded upon it.

Parr is said on one occasion to have called for a pipe after taking a meal at a coaching-inn called the "Bush" at Bristol, when the waiter told him that smoking was not allowed at the Bush. Parr persisted, but the authorities at the inn were firm in their refusal to allow anything so vulgar as smoking on their premises, where-upon Parr is said to have exclaimed: "Why, man, I've smoked in the dining-room of every nobleman in England. The Duchess of Devonshire said I could smoke in every room in her house but her dressing-room, and here, in this dirty public-house of Bristol you forbid smoking! Amazing! Bring me my bill." The learned doctor exaggerated no doubt as regards the facilities given him for smoking; for it was his overbearing way not to ask for leave to smoke, but to smoke wherever he went, whether invited to do so or not; but the story shows the prejudice against smoking which was found in many places as a result of the attitude of the fashionable world towards tobacco.

Johnstone, Parr's biographer, referring to his hero's failure to obtain prefer-ment to the Episcopal Bench about the year 1804, says--"His pipe might be deemed in these fantastic days a degradation at the table of the palace or the castle; but his noble hospitality, combined with his habits of sobriety, whether tobacco fumigated his table or not, would have filled his hall with the learned and the good." A por-trait of Parr hangs in the Combination Room in St. John's, Cambridge. Originally it represented him faithfully with a long clay between hand and mouth; but for some unknown reason the pipe has been painted out.

A famous crony of Parr's, the learned Porson, was another devotee of tobacco. In November 1789 Parr wrote to Dr. Burney: "The books may be consulted, and

Porson shall do it, and he will do it. I know his price when he bargains with me; two bottles instead of one, six pipes instead of two, burgundy instead of claret, liberty to sit till five in the morning instead of sneaking into bed at one: these are his terms:" and these few lines, it may be added, give a graphic picture of Porson. According to Maltby, Porson once remarked that when smoking began to go out of fashion, learning began to go out of fashion also--which shows what nonsense a learned man could talk.

Another famous parson, the Rev. John Newton, was a smoker, and so was Cowper's other clerical friend, that learned and able Dissenter, the Rev. William Bull, whose whole mien and bearing were so dignified that on two occasions he was mistaken for a bishop. Cowper appreciated snuff, but did not care for smoking, and when he wrote to Unwin, describing his new-made friend in terms of admiration, he concluded--"Such a man is Mr. Bull. But--he smokes tobacco. Nothing is perfection 'Nihil est ab omni parte beatum.'" Bull, however, was not excessive in his smoking, for his daily allowance was but three pipes. In his garden at Newport Pagnell, Bull showed Cowper a nook in which he had placed a bench, where he said he found it very refreshing to smoke his pipe and meditate. "Here he sits," wrote Cowper, "with his back against one brick wall, and his nose against another, which must, you know, be very refreshing, and greatly assist meditation."

Cowper's aversion from tobacco could not have been very strong, for he encouraged his friend to smoke in the famous Summer House at Olney, which was the poet's outdoor study. Bull smoked Orinoco tobacco, which he carried in one of the tobacco-boxes, which in those days were much more commonly used than pouches, and this box on one occasion he accidentally left behind him at Olney. Cowper returned it to him with the well-known rhymed epistle dated June 22, 1782, and beginning:

If reading verse be your delight,
'Tis mine as much, or more, to write;
But what we would, so weak is man,
Lies oft remote from what we can.

He describes the box and its contents in lines which show not only tolerance but appreciation of tobacco, from which it is not unreasonable to infer that Cowper's first view of his friend's smoking-habit as a drawback--as shown in his letter to Unwin, quoted above--had been modified by neighbourhood and custom. It might have been well for the poet himself if he had learned to smoke a social pipe with his friend Bull. The appreciative lines run thus:

> *This oval box well filled*
> *With best tobacco, finely milled,*
> *Beats all Anticyra's pretences*
> *To disengage the encumbered senses.*
> * O Nymph of transatlantic fame,*
> *Where'er thine haunt, whate'er thy name,*
> *Whether reposing on the side*
> *Of Oronoco's spacious tide,*
> *Or listening with delight not small*
> *To Niagara's distant fall,*
> *'Tis thine to cherish and to feed*
> *The pungent nose-refreshing weed,*
> *Which, whether pulverized it gain*
> *A speedy passage to the brain,*
> *Or whether, touched with fire, it rise*
> *In circling eddies to the skies,*
> *Does thought more quicken and refine*
> *Than all the breath of all the Nine--*
> *Forgive the bard, if bard he be,*
> *Who once too wantonly made free,*
> *To touch with a satiric wipe*
> *That symbol of thy power, the pipe;*
> *   *   *   *   *   *
>
> *And so may smoke-inhaling Bull*
> *Be always filling, never full.*

The allusion in these verses to a "satiric wipe" refers to a passage in the poem entitled "Conversation," which Cowper had written in the previous year, 1781. In this passage tobacco is abused in terms which Cowper clearly felt to need modification after his personal intercourse with such a smoker as his friend Bull. In describing, in "Conversation," the manner in which a story is sometimes told, the poet says:

> *The pipe, with solemn interposing puff,*
> *Makes half a sentence at a time enough;*
> *The dozing sages drop the drowsy strain,*
> *Then pause and puff--and speak, and pause again.*
> *Such often, like the tube they so admire,*
> *Important triflers! have more smoke than fire.*

Cowper then goes on to attack tobacco in lines which show how unpopular smoking at that date was with ladies, and which have since often been quoted by anti-tobacconists with grateful appreciation:

> *Pernicious weed! whose scent the fair annoys,*
> *Unfriendly to society's chief joys,*
> *Thy worst effect is banishing for hours*
> *The sex whose presence civilizes ours;*
> *Thou art indeed the drug a gardener wants,*
> *To poison vermin that infest his plants,*
> *But are we so to wit and beauty blind,*
> *As to despise the glory of our kind,*
> *And show the softest minds and fairest forms*
> *As little mercy as the grubs and worms?*

Notwithstanding this "satiric wipe," it is not likely that Cowper would have had much sympathy with John Wesley, who, in his detestation of what had been his father's solace at Epworth, forbade his preachers either to smoke or to take snuff.

In the first two or three decades of the nineteenth century smoking reached its nadir. No dandy smoked. If some witnesses may be believed smoking had almost died out even at Oxford. Archdeacon Denison wrote in his "Memories"--"When I went up to Oxford, 1823-24, there were two things unknown in Christ Church, and I believe very generally in Oxford--smoking and slang"; but one cannot help fancying that the archdeacon's memory was not quite trustworthy. It is difficult to imagine that there was ever a time when the slang of the day was not current on the lips of young Oxford, or that so long as tobacco was procurable it did not find its way into college rooms.

If smoking had died out at Oxford its decline must have been rapid. When a certain young John James was an undergraduate of Queen's, 1778 to 1781, he and his correspondents spoke severely of the "miserable condition of Fellows who (under the liberal pretence of educating youth) spend half their lives in smoking tobacco and reading the newspapers." About 1800 the older or more old-fashioned of the Fellows at New College, "not liking the then newly introduced luxury of Turkey carpets," says Mr. G.V. Cox, in his "Recollections of Oxford," 1868, "often adjourned to smoke their pipe in a little room opposite to the Senior Common-room, now appropriated to other uses, but then kept as a smoking-room." A Mr. Rhodes, a one-time Fellow of Worcester College, who was elected Esquire Bedel in Medicine and Arts in 1792, had a very peculiar way of enjoying his tobacco. Mr. Cox says: "On one occasion, when I had to call upon him, I found him drinking rum and water, and enjoying (what he called his luxury) the fumes of tobacco, not through a pipe or in the shape of a cigar, but burnt in a dish!"

Smoking had certainly not died out at Cambridge, even at the time when Denison was at Oxford. According to the "Gradus ad Cantabrigium," 1824, the Cambridge smart man's habit was to dine in the evening "at his own rooms, or at those of a friend, and afterwards blows a cloud, puffs at a segar, and drinks copiously." The spelling of "segar" shows that cigars were then somewhat of a novelty.

When Tennyson was an undergraduate at Cambridge, 1828-30, he and his companions all smoked. At the meetings of the "Apostles"--the little group of friends which included the future Laureate--"much coffee was drunk, much tobacco smoked." Dons smoked as well as undergraduates. At Queens', the Combination-room in Tennyson's time had still a sanded floor, and the "table was set handsomely forth with long 'churchwardens'"--as the poet told Palgrave when the two visited Cambridge in 1859. George Pryme, in his "Autobiographic Recollections," 1870, states that in 1800 "smoking was allowed in the Trinity Combination-room after supper in the twelve days of Christmas, when a few old men availed themselves of it," which looks as if tobacco were not very popular just then at Trinity. With the wine, pipes and the large silver tobacco-box were laid on the table. Porson, when asked for an inscription for the box, suggested "+To bakcho+." Pryme says that among the undergraduates, of whom he was one, tobacco had no favour, and "an attempt of Mr. Ginkell, son of Lord Athlone ... to introduce smoking at his own wine-parties failed, although he had the prestige of being a hat-fellow-commoner."

No doubt smoking had its ups and downs at the Universities apart from the set of the main current of fashion. We learn from the invaluable Gunning that at Cambridge about 1786 smoking was going "out of fashion among the junior members of our combination-rooms, except on the river in the evening, when every man put a short pipe in his mouth." "I took great pains," he adds, "to make myself master of this elegant accomplishment, but I never succeeded, though I used to renew the attempt with a perseverance worthy of a better cause." About the same time Dr. Farmer was Master of Emmanuel and the Master was an inveterate smoker. Gunning says that Emmanuel parlour under Farmer's presidency was always open to those who loved pipes and tobacco and cheerful conversation--a very natural collocation of tastes. Farmer's silver tobacco-pipe is still preserved in his old college, while Porson's japanned snuff-box is at Trinity.

Dr. Farmer was elected Master of Emmanuel in 1775. Years before he had held the curacy of Swavesey, about nine miles out of Cambridge, where he regularly performed the duty. After morning service it was his custom to repair to the local public-house where he enjoyed a mutton-chop and potatoes. Immediately after the removal of the cloth, "Mr. Dobson (his churchwarden) and one or two of the principal farmers, made their appearance, to whom he invariably said, 'I am going to read prayers, but shall be back by the time you have made the punch.' Occasionally another farmer accompanied him from church, when pipes and tobacco"--with the punch--"were in requisition until 6 o'clock." The Sabbath afternoon thus satisfactorily concluded, Farmer returned to college in Cambridge and took a nap, till at nine he went to the parlour of the college where the Fellows usually assembled, and pipes and tobacco concluded a well-spent day.

In the fashionable world the snuff-box was all-powerful. The Prince Regent was devoted to snuff, but disdained tobacco. He had a "cellar of snuff," which after his death was sold, said John Bull, August 15, 1830, "to a well-known purveyor, for L400." Lord Petersham, famous among dandies, made a wonderful collection of snuffs and snuff-boxes, and was curious in his choice of a box to carry. Gronow relates that once when a light Sevres snuff-box which Lord Petersham was using, was admired, the noble owner replied, with a gentle lisp--"Yes, it is a nice summer box--but would certainly be inappropriate for winter wear!" The well-known purveyor who bought the Prince Regent's cellar of snuff, and who bought also Lord Petersham's stock, was the Fribourg of Fribourg and Treyer, whose well-known old-fashioned shop at the top of the Haymarket, with a bow-window on each side of the door, still gives an eighteenth-century flavour to that thoroughfare. All the dandies of the period were connoisseurs of snuff, and imitated the royal mirror of fashion in their devotion to the scented powder. Young Charles Stanhope wrote to his brother on November 5, 1812--"I have learnt to take snuff among other fashionable acquirements, a custom which, of course, you have learnt and will be able to keep me in countenance." But no dandies or young men of fashion smoked. Tobacco, save in the disguise of snuff, was tabooed.

Smoking was frowned upon, even in places where hitherto it had been allowed. In 1812 the authorities of Sion College ordered "that Coffee and Tea be provided in the Parlour for the Visitors and Incumbents, and in the Court Room for the Curates and Lecturers; and that Pipes and Tobacco be not allowed; and that no Wine be at any time carried into the Court Room, nor any into the Hall after Coffee and Tea shall have been ordered on that day."

The use of tobacco for smoking, as I have said, had reached its nadir--in the fashionable world, that is to say--but the dawn follows the darkest hour, and the revival of smoking was at hand, thanks to the cigar.

IX
SIGNS OF REVIVAL

Some sigh for this and that
My wishes don't go far;
The world may wag at will,
So I have my cigar.
THOMAS HOOD.

The revival of smoking among those who were most amenable to the dictates of fashion, and among whom consequently tobacco had long been in bad odour, came by way of the cigar.

In the preceding chapters all the references to and illustrations of smoking have been concerned with pipes. Until the early years of the nineteenth century the use of cigars was practically unknown in this country. The earliest notices of cigars in English books occur in accounts of travel in Spain and Portugal, and in the Spanish Colonies, and in such notices the phonetic spelling of "segar" often occurs. A few folk still cling to this spelling--there was a "segar-shop" in the Strand till quite recently, and I saw the notice "segars" the other day over a small tobacco-shop in York--which has no authority, and on etymological grounds is indefensible. The derivation of "cigar" is not altogether clear; but the probabilities are strongly in favour of its connexion with "cigarra," the Spanish name for the cicada, the shrilly-chirping insect familiar in the southern countries of Europe, and the subject of frequent allusions by the ancient writers of Greece and Rome, as well as by modern scribes. A Spanish lexicographer of authority says that the cigar has the form of a "cicada" of paper, and, on the whole, it is highly probable that the likeness of the roll of tobacco-leaf to the cylindrical body of the insect (cigarra) was the reason that the "cigarro" was so called. There is no warrant of any kind for "segar."

The earliest mention of cigars in English occurs in a book dated 1735. A traveller in Spanish America, named Cockburn, whose narrative was published in that year, describes how he met three friars at Nicaragua, who, he says, "gave us some Seegars to smoke ... these are Leaves of Tobacco rolled up in such Manner that they serve both for a Pipe and Tobacco itself ... they know no other way here, for there is no such Thing as a Tobacco-Pipe throughout New Spain."

Cheroots seem to have been known somewhat earlier. The earliest mention of them is dated about 1670. Sir James Murray, in the great Oxford Dictionary, gives the following interesting extract from an unpublished MS. relating to India, written between 1669 and 1679: "The Poore Sort of Inhabitants vizt. yet Gentues, Mallabars, &c., Smoke theire Tobacco after a very meane, but I judge Original manner, Onely ye leafe rowled up, and light one end, holdinge ye other between their lips ... this is called a bunko, and by ye Portugals a Cheroota." The condemnation of cheroot-or cigar-smoking as a mean method of taking tobacco has an odd look in the light of modern habits and customs.

The use of cigars in this country began to come in early in the last century; and by at least 1830 they were being freely, if privately, smoked. It is probable that the reduction of the duty on cigars from 18s. to 9s. a lb., in 1829, had its effect in making cigars more popular. Croker, in 1831, commenting on Johnson's saying that smoking had gone out, said: "The taste for smoking, however, has revived, probably from the military habits of Europe during the French wars; but instead of the sober sedentary pipe, the ambulatory cigar is chiefly used." Croker's shrewd suggestion was probably not far wide of the truth. It is quite likely, if not highly probable, that the revival of smoking in the shape of the cigar was directly connected with the experiences of British officers in Spain and Portugal during the Peninsular War.

One of the earliest cigar-smokers must have been that remarkable clergyman, the Rev. Charles Caleb Colton, whose "Lacon," published in 1820, was once popular. Colton was in succession Rector of Tiverton and Vicar of Kew, but on leaving Kew became a wine-merchant in Soho. While at Kew he is said to have kept cigars under the pulpit, where, he said, the temperature was exactly right.

At first even cigar-smoking was confined to comparatively few persons, and the social prejudice against tobacco continued unabated. Thackeray significantly makes

Rawdon Crawley a smoker--the action of "Vanity Fair" takes place in the first two decades of the nineteenth century. The original smoking-room of the Athenaeum Club, which was founded in 1824, the present building being erected in 1830, was a miserable little room, Dr. Hawtree, on behalf of the committee, announcing that "no gentleman smoked." The Oriental Club, when built in 1826-27, contained no smoking-room at all.

Sir Walter Scott often smoked cigars, though he seems to have regarded it in the light of an indulgence to be half-apologized for. In his "Journal," July 4, 1829, he noted--"When I had finished my bit of dinner, and was in a quiet way smoking my cigar over a glass of negus, Adam Ferguson comes with a summons to attend him to the Justice Clerk's, where, it seems, I was engaged. I was totally out of case to attend his summons, redolent as I was of tobacco. But I am vexed at the circumstance. It looks careless, and, what is worse, affected; and the Justice is an old friend more-over." Tobacco in any form was suspect. A man might smoke a cigar, but he must not take the odour into the drawing-room of even an old friend.

A few years earlier, in November 1825, Scott had written in his "Journal" that after dinner he usually smoked a couple of cigars which operated as a sedative--

Just to drive the cold winter away,   And drown the fatigues of the day.

"I smoked a good deal," he continued, "about twenty years ago when at Ashes-tiel; but, coming down one morning to the parlour, I found, as the room was small and confined, that the smell was unpleasant, and laid aside the use of the Nicotian weed for many years; but was again led to use it by the example of my son, a hussar officer, and my son-in-law, an Oxford student. I could lay it aside to-morrow; I laugh at the dominion of custom in this and many things.

"We make the giants first, and then *do not* kill them."

Scott's remark that Lockhart smoked when an Oxford student rather discredits Archdeacon's Denison's statement, quoted in the preceding chapter, that smoking was very generally unknown in Oxford in 1823-24. The archdeacon was writing from memory--a very untrustworthy recorder; Scott's remark was that of a con-temporary.

Byron is reputed to have been another cigar-smoker. His apostrophe to tobacco in "The Island" (1823), a poem founded in part on the history of the Mutiny of the Bounty, is familiar. The lines are, indeed, almost the only familiar passage in that poem:

> Sublime tobocco! which, from east to west,
> Cheers the tar's labours or the Turkman's rest;
> Which on the Moslem's ottoman divides
> His hours, and rivals opium and his brides;
> Magnificent in Stamboul, but less grand,
> Though not less loved, in Wapping or the Strand:
> Divine in hookas, glorious in a pipe,
> When tipp'd with amber, mellow, rich, and ripe;
> Like other charmers, wooing the caress,
> More dazzlingly when daring in full dress;
> Yet thy true lovers more admire by far
> Thy naked beauties--Give me a cigar!

How far these lines really represent the poet's own sentiments, and whether he habitually smoked either cigar or pipe, is another matter.

Other men of letters of the time were zealous adherents of the pipe. One of these was the poet Campbell. From 1820 to 1830 he was editor of the New Monthly Magazine, and is reputed to have been so very unbusinesslike in his methods that there was always difficulty in getting proofs corrected and returned in good time. On one occasion, as reported by a member of the firm that printed the magazine, a proof had been lost, and the poet was informed that the article must go to press next day uncorrected. Campbell sent word that he would look in in the morning and correct it. Preparations were duly made to receive him; he was shown into the best room, and left with the proof on his table. After a while he rang the bell, and said, "I could do this much better if I had a pipe." Thereupon pipe and tobacco were procured and taken in to him. Campbell tore open the paper containing the tobacco, and, with a slightly contemptuous expression, exclaimed, "Ugh! C'naster! I'd rather it had been shag!"

Charles Lamb was a heavy pipe-smoker. He smoked too much--regretted it-- but continued to smoke, not wisely but too well. "He came home very smoky and drinky last night," says his sister of him.

When sending some books to Coleridge at Keswick in November 1802, Lamb wrote--"If you find the Miltons in certain parts dirtied and soiled with a crumb of right Gloucester, blacked in the candle (my usual supper), or peradventure, a stray ash of tobacco wafted into the crevices, look to that passage more especially: depend upon it, it contains good matter." To Lamb, a book read best over a pipe.

The following year he wrote to Coleridge--"What do you think of smoking? I want your sober, average, noon opinion, of it. I generally am eating my dinner about the time I should determine it. Morning is a girl, and can't smoke--she's no evidence one way or the other; and Night is so evidently bought over, he can't be a very upright judge. Maybe the truth is that one *pipe is wholesome,* two *pipes toothsome,* three *pipes noisome,* four *pipes fulsome,* five *pipes quarrelsome, and that's the* sum on't. But that is deciding rather upon rhyme than reason.... After all, our instincts may be best." It is clear from one or two references, that Lamb and Coleridge had been accustomed to smoke together at their meetings in early days at the "Salutation and Cat"--with less disastrous results to Coleridge, it is to be hoped, than those which followed his Birmingham smoke, as set forth in the preceding chapter.

In 1805 Lamb wrote to Wordsworth--"now I have bid farewell to my 'sweet enemy' tobacco ... I shall, perhaps, set nobly to work." Forthwith he set to work on the farce "Mr. H.," which some months later was produced at Drury Lane and was promptly damned. After its failure Lamb wrote to Hazlitt--"We are determined not to be cast down. I am going to leave off tobacco, and then we must thrive. A smoky man must write smoky farces." But Lamb and his pipe were not to be parted by even repeated resolutions to leave off smoking. It was years after this that he met Macready at Talfourd's, and by way probably of saying something to shock Macready; whose personality could hardly have been sympathetic to him, uttered the remarkable wish that the last breath he drew in might be through a pipe and exhaled in a pun.

It was in 1818 that Lamb published the collection of his writings, in two volumes, which contained the well-known "Farewell to Tobacco," written in 1805, and referred to in the letter of that year to Wordsworth quoted above. Its phrases of mingled abuse and affection are familiar to lovers of Lamb.

Parr is reported to have once asked Lamb how he could smoke so much and so fast, and Lamb is said to have replied--"I toiled after it, sir, as some men toil after virtue." But if all accounts are true, Parr far outsmoked Lamb. If the essayist discontinued or modified his smoking habits, he made up for it by devotion to snuff--a devotion which his sister shared. A large snuff-box usually lay on the table between them, and they pushed it one to the other.

But it is time to return to the cigar, and the changing attitude of fashion towards smoking.

There would appear to have been some smokers who disliked the new-fangled cigars. Angelo seems, from various passages in his "Reminiscences," to have been a smoker, and to have been very frequently in the company of smokers, yet he could write: "There are few things which, after a foreign tour, more forcibly remind us that we are again in England, than the superiority of our stage-coaches. There is something very exhilarating in being carried through the air with rapidity ... considering the rate at which stage-coaches now travel [i.e. in and just before 1830] ... a place on the box or front of a prime set-out is, indeed, a considerable treat. But alas! no human enjoyment is free from alloy. A Jew pedlar or mendicant foreigner with his cigar in his mouth, has it in his power to turn the draft of sweet air into a cup of bitterness." Perhaps Angelo's objection was more to the quality of the cigar that would be smoked by a "Jew pedlar or mendicant foreigner," than to the cigar itself. Yet, going on to describe a journey to Hastings, sitting "on the roof in front" beside an acquaintance, he says, notwithstanding the enjoyment of dashing along, anecdote and jest going merrily on, "we had the annoyance of a coxcomb perched on the box, infecting the fresh air which Heaven had sent us, with the smoke of his abominable cigar," which looks as if his real objection was to cigars, as such.

The fashionable dislike of tobacco-smoke appears in the pages of another descriptive writer--the once well known N.P. Willis, the American author of many books of travel and gossip. In his "Pencillings by the Way," writing in July 1833, Willis describes the prevalence of smoking in Vienna among all the nationalities that thronged that cosmopolitan capital. "It is," he says, "like a fancy ball. Hungarians, Poles, Croats, Wallachians, Jews, Moldavians, Greeks, Turks, all dressed in their national and stinking costumes, promenade up and down, smoking all, and none exciting the slightest observation. Every third window is a pipe-shop, and they [presumably the pipes] show, by their splendour and variety, the expensiveness of the passion. Some of them are marked '200 dollars.' The streets reek with tobacco-smoke. You never catch a breath of untainted air within the Glacis. Your hotel, your cafe, your coach, your friend, are all redolent of the same disgusting odour." In the following year, describing a large dinner-party at the Duke of Gordon's in Scotland, Willis says that when the ladies left the table, the gentlemen closed up and "conversation assumed a merrier cast," then "coffee and liqueurs were brought in, when the wines began to be circulated more slowly," and at eleven o'clock there was a general move to the drawing-room. The dinner began at seven, so the guests had been four hours at table; but smoking is not mentioned, and it is quite certain from Willis's silence on the subject--the "disgusting odour" would surely have disturbed him--that no single member of the large dinner-party dreamed of smoking, or, at all events, attempted to smoke.

By 1830 smoking had so far "come in" again that a considerable proportion of the members of the House of Commons were smokers. Macaulay has drawn for us the not very attractive picture of the smoking-room of the old House of Commons--before the fire of 1834--in a letter to his sister dated in the summer of 1831. "I have left Sir Francis Burdett on his legs," he wrote, "and repaired to the smoking-room; a large, wainscoted, uncarpeted place, with tables covered with green baize and writing materials. On a full night it is generally thronged towards twelve o'clock with smokers. It is then a perfect cloud of fume. There have I seen (tell it not to the West Indians), Buxton blowing fire out of his mouth. My father will not believe it. At present, however, all the doors and windows are open, and the room is pure enough from tobacco to suit my father himself." In July 1832 he again dated a letter to his sisters from the House of Commons smoking-room. "I am writing here," he says, "at eleven at night, in this filthiest of all filthy atmospheres ... with the smell of tobacco in my nostrils.... Reject not my letter, though it is redolent of cigars and genuine pigtail; for this is the room--

The room,--but I think I'll describe it in rhyme,
That smells of tobacco and chloride of lime.
 The smell of tobacco was always the same:
But the chloride was bought since the cholera came."

The mention of pigtail shows that the House contained pipe- as well as cigar-smokers. A few days later he wrote again to his sisters, but this time from the library, where, he says, "we are in a far better atmosphere than in the smoking-room, whence I wrote to you last week." One wonders why Macaulay, who apparently did not smoke himself, and who, though somewhat more tolerant of tobacco than his father, Zachary Macaulay, evidently did not like the atmosphere of the smoking-room, chose to write there, when the library--where he must surely have felt more at home--was available.

Among other well-known men of standing and fashion who were smokers about this period may be named Lord Eldon, Lord Stowell, Brougham, Lord Calthorp and H.R.H. the Duke of Sussex. In Thackeray's "Book of Snobs," Miss Wirt, the governess at Major Ponto's, refers in shocked tones to "H.R.H. the poor dear Duke of Sussex (such a man my dears, but alas! addicted to smoking!)."

Sad to say, the Royal Duke was not content with the cigar that was becoming fashionable, but actually smoked a pipe. Mrs. Stirling, in "The Letter-Bag of Lady Elizabeth Spencer-Stanhope," 1913, notes that Lord Althorp was a frequent visitor about 1822 at Holkham, the well-known seat of Mr. Coke of Norfolk, later Lord Leicester, and that on such occasions he enjoyed "the distinction of being the only guest besides the Duke of Sussex who ever indulged in the rare habit of smoking. But while the Royal Duke was wont to puff away at a long meerschaum in his bedroom till he actually blinded himself, and all who came near him, Fidele Jack [Lord Althorp's nickname] behaved in more considerate fashion, only smoking out of doors as he passed restlessly up and down the grass terrace."

With the revival of smoking, things changed at Holkham. On Christmas Day, 1847, Lady Elizabeth, writing to her husband from Holkham, the home of her childhood, remarked: "The Billiard table is always lighted up for the gentlemen when they come from shooting, and there they sit smoking."

The growing popularity of the cigar made smoking less unfashionable than it had been among the upper classes of society; but among humbler folk pipe-smoking had never "gone out." Every public-house did its regular trade in clays, known as churchwardens and Broseleys, and by other names either of familiarity or descriptive of the place of manufacture; and on the mantelpiece or table of inn or ale-house stood the tobacco-box. Miss Jekyll, in her delightful book on "Old West Surrey," figures an example of these old public-house tobacco-boxes which is made of lead. It has bosses of lions' heads at the ends, and a portrait in relief on the front of the Duke of Wellington in his plumed cocked hat. Inside, there is a flat piece of sheet-lead with a knob to keep the tobacco pressed close, so that it may not dry up.

A curious and popular variety of tobacco-box often to be found in rural inns and ale-houses was made somewhat on the principle of the now everywhere familiar automatic machines. The late Mr. Frederick Gale, in a column of "Tobacco Reminiscences," which he contributed to the Globe newspaper in 1899, said, that at village outdoor festivals of the 'thirties and early 'forties, respectable elderly farmers and tradesmen would sit "round a table, on which was an automatic, square, brass tobacco-box of large dimensions, into which the smokers dropped a halfpenny and the lid flew back, and the publican trusted to the smoker's honour to fill his pipe and close the box." When the pipes were filled they were lighted by means of tinder-box and flint, and a stable lanthorn supplied by the ostler. A penny would appear to have been a more usual charge, for a frequent inscription on the lid was:

> The custom is, before you fill,
> To put a penny in the till;
> When you have filled, without delay
> Close the lid, or sixpence pay.

One of these old brass penny-in-the-slot tobacco-boxes was included in the exhibition of Welsh Antiquities held at Cardiff in the summer of 1913.

In the Colchester Museum is an automatic tobacco-box and till of japanned iron. On the lid of the box is painted a keg of tobacco and two clay pipes; and on that of the till the following doggerel lines:

> A halfpeny dropt into the till,
> Upsprings the lid and you may fill;
> When you have filled, without delay,
> Shut down the lid, or sixpence pay.

A correspondent of Notes and Queries, in 1908, mentioned that he possessed two of these old penny-in-the-slot tobacco-boxes, and had come across another in a dealer's shop of a somewhat peculiar make, about which he wished to get information. "It is of the ordinary shape," he wrote, "but differs from any I have previously seen in this respect, that it works with a sixpence, and not with a penny or halfpenny. It is engraved with the usual lines, except that the user is asked to put sixpence in the till, and then to shut down the lid under penalty of a fine of a shilling. What could it have been used for that was worth sixpence a time? Other uncommon features are that the money portion is shallow, and that the part for the tobacco extends the whole length of the box. I should say that the box is much smaller than any others I have ever seen." No information as to the use of this curious box was forthcoming from any of the learned and ingenious correspondents of Notes and Queries; and a problem which they cannot solve may not unreasonably be regarded as insoluble.

Readers of Dickens are familiar with the drawing by Cruikshank which illustrates the chapter on "Scotland Yard" in Dickens's "Sketches by Boz," which was written before 1836. It shows the coal-heavers sitting round the fire shouting out "some sturdy chorus," and smoking long clays. "Here," wrote Dickens, "in a dark wainscoted-room of ancient appearance, cheered by the glow of a mighty fire ... sat the lusty coal-heavers, quaffing large draughts of Barclay's best, and puffing forth volumes of smoke, which wreathed heavily above their heads, and involved the room in a thick dark cloud." These good folk and others of their kin had never been affected by any change of fashion in respect of smoking. In another of the "Sketches," the amusing "Tuggs's at Ramsgate," when poor Cymon Tuggs is hid behind the curtain, half dead with fear, he hears Captain Waters call for brandy and cigars--"The cigars were introduced; the captain was a professed smoker; so was the lieutenant; so was Joseph Tuggs." Poor Cymon, on the other hand, was one of those who could never smoke "without feeling it indispensably necessary to retire, immediately, and never could smell smoke without a strong disposition to cough." Consequently, as the apartment was small, the door closed and the smoke powerful, poor Cymon was soon compelled to cough, which precipitated the catastrophe. It is noticeable that Dickens speaks of the three worthies as professed smokers, a remark which suggests that such dare-devils, men who would take cigars as a matter of course and for enjoyment, and not merely out of a complimentary acquiescence in some one else's wish, were comparatively rare.

Other illustrations of folk who smoked, not cigars, but pipes, may be drawn from "Pickwick," which was published in 1836. At the very beginning, when Mr. Pickwick calls a cab at Saint Martin's-le-Grand, the first cab is "fetched from the public-house, where he had been smoking his first pipe." At Rochester, Mr. Pickwick makes notes on the four towns of Strood, Rochester, Chatham and Brompton, where the military were present in strength, and hence the observant gentleman noted--"The consumption of tobacco in these towns must be very great: and the smell which pervades the streets must be exceedingly delicious to those who are extremely fond of smoking." On the evening of the election at Eatanswill, Tupman and Snodgrass resort to the commercial room of the Peacock Inn, where "the atmosphere was redolent of tobacco-smoke, the fumes of which had communicated a rather dingy hue to the whole room, and more especially to the dusty red curtains which shaded the windows." Here, among others, were the dirty-faced man with a clay pipe, the very red-faced man behind a cigar, and the man with a black eye, who slowly filled a large Dutch pipe with most capacious bowl. Tupman and Snodgrass were of the company and smoked cigars. Sam Weller's father smoked his pipe philosophically. If Sam's "mother-in-law" "flies in a passion, and breaks his pipe, he steps out and gets another. Then she screams wery loud, and falls into 'sterics; and he smokes wery comfortably 'till she comes to agin." What better example could there be of pipe-engendered philosophy? When Mr. Pickwick and Sam look in at old Weller's house of call off Cheapside, they find the boxes full of stage coachmen, drinking and smoking, and among them is the old gentleman himself, "smoking with great vehemence." After having given his son valuable parental advice, "Mr. Weller, senior, refilled his pipe from a tin box he carried in his pocket, and, lighting his fresh pipe from the ashes of the old one, commenced smoking at a great rate."

A little later when Mr. Pickwick hunts up Perker's clerk Lowten, and joins the jovial circle at the Magpie and Stump, he finds on his right hand "a gentleman in a checked shirt and Mosaic studs, with a cigar in his mouth," who expresses the hope that the newcomer does not "find this sort of thing disagreeable." "Not in the least," replied Mr. Pickwick, "I like it very much, although I am no smoker myself." "I should be very sorry to say I wasn't," interposes another gentleman on the opposite side of the table. "It's board and lodging to me, is smoke." Mr. Pickwick glances at the speaker, and thinks that if it were washing too, it would be all the better!

Later again when the "couple o' Sawbones," the medical students, Ben Allen and Bob Sawyer, make their first appearance on the scene, they are discovered in the morning seated by Mr. Wardle's kitchen fire, smoking cigars; and it is significant of how smoking out of doors was then regarded that Dickens, going on to describe Sawyer in detail, refers to "that sort of slovenly smartness, and swaggering gait, which is peculiar to young gentlemen who smoke in the streets by day, shout and scream in the same by night, call waiters by their Christian names, and do various other acts and deeds of an equally facetious description." Apparently in 1836 the only person who would allow himself to be seen smoking in the street was of the kind naturally inclined to do the other objectionable things mentioned. The same idea runs through the allusions to tobacco in "Pickwick." Smoking was undeniably vulgar. Mr. John Smauker, who introduces Sam Weller at the "friendly swarry" of the Bath footmen, smokes a cigar "through an amber tube"--cigar-holders were a novelty. When Mr. Pickwick is taken to the house of Namby, the sheriffs' officer, the "principal features" of the front parlour are "fresh sand and stale tobacco smoke." One of the occupants of the room is a "mere boy of nineteen or twenty, who, though it was yet barely ten o'clock, was drinking gin and water, and smoking a cigar, amusements to which, judging from his inflamed countenance, he had devoted himself pretty constantly for the last year or two of his life." Tobacco-smoke pervades the Fleet prison. In fact, to trace tobacco through the pages of "Pickwick" is to realize vividly how vulgar if not vicious an accomplishment smoking was considered by the fashionable world and how popular it was among the nobodies of the unfashionable world.

Similar morals may be drawn from other works of fiction. The action of the first chapters of Thackeray's "Pendennis" passes early in the nineteenth century. In the third chapter Foker has a cigar in his mouth as he strolls with Pen down the High Street of Chatteris. Old Doctor Portman meets them and regards "with wonder Pen's friend, from whose mouth and cigar clouds of fragrance issued, which curled round the doctor's honest face and shovel hat. 'An old school-fellow of mine, Mr. Foker,' said Pen. The doctor said 'H'm!' and scowled at the cigar. He did not mind a pipe in his study, but the cigar was an abomination to the worthy gentleman." The reverend gentleman in liking his pipe was faithful to the traditional fondness for smoking of parsons; but smoking must be in the study. To smoke in the street was vulgar; and to smoke the newfangled cigar was worse.

Pendennis, when he comes home the first time from Oxbridge, brings with him a large box of cigars of strange brand, which he smokes "not only about the stables and greenhouses, where they were good" for his mother's plants, and which were obviously places to which a man who wished to smoke should betake himself, but in his own study, which rather shocks his mother. Pen goes from bad to worse during his University days, and, sad to say, one Sunday in the last long vacation, the "wretched boy," instead of going to church, "was seen at the gate of the Clavering Arms smoking a cigar, in the face of the congregation as it issued from St. Mary's. There was an awful sensation in the village society. Portman prophesied Pen's ruin after that, and groaned in spirit over the rebellious young prodigal." Later the smoke from Warrington's short pipe and Pen's cigars floats through many pages of the novel.

X
EARLY VICTORIAN DAYS

Scent to match thy rich perfume
Chemic art did ne'er presume
Through her quaint alembic strain,
None so sovereign to the brain.
  LAMB, A Farewell to Tobacco.

The social attitude towards smoking in early Victorian days, and for some time later, was curious. The development of cigar-smoking among those classes from which tobacco had long been practically banished, and the natural consequent spread downwards of the use of cigars--in accordance with the invariable law of fashion--together with the continued devotion to the pipe among those whose love of tobacco had never slackened, made smoking a much more general practice than it had been for some generations.

It is somewhat significant that Dickens, in the "Old Curiosity Shop," 1840, makes that repulsive dwarf, Quilp, smoke cigars. When the little monster comes home unexpectedly in the fourth chapter of the book, and breaks up his wife's tea-party, he settles himself in an arm-chair--"with his large head and face squeezed up against the back, and his little legs planted on the table"--with a case-bottle of rum, cold water, and a box of cigars before him. "Now, Mrs. Quilp," he says, "I feel in a smoking humour, and shall probably blaze away all night. But sit where you are, if you please, in case I want you." Quilp smokes cigars one after the other, his wretched wife sitting patiently by, from sunset till some time after daybreak. The dwarf's tastes, however, were catholic. A little later in the book the reader finds him, when encamped in the back parlour of the old man's shop, smoking pipe after pipe, and compelling that knavish attorney, Sampson Brass, to do the same. Tobacco-smoke always caused Brass "great internal discomposure and annoyance"; but this made no difference to Quilp, who insisted on his "friend" continuing to smoke, while he inquired: "Is it good, Brass, is it nice, is it fragrant, do you feel like the Grand Turk?" But Quilp and Brass were not in "society."

Notwithstanding that the number of smokers had so largely increased, and was continually increasing, smoking was regarded socially as something of a vice--to be practised in inconvenient places and not too publicly.

There were still plenty of active opponents and denouncers of tobacco. One of the most distinguished was the great Duke of Wellington, who abominated smoking, and was annoyed by the increase of cigar-smoking among officers of the army. In the early 'forties he issued a General Order (No. 577) which contained a paragraph that would have delighted the heart of King James I. It ran thus: "The Commander-in-Chief has been informed, that the practice of smoking, by the use of pipes, cigars, or cheroots, has become prevalent among the Officers of the Army, which is not only in itself a species of intoxication occasioned by the fumes of tobacco, but, undoubtedly, occasions drinking and tippling by those who acquire the habit; and he intreats the Officers commanding Regiments to prevent smoking in the Mess Rooms of their several Regiments, and in the adjoining apartments, and to discourage the practice among the Officers of Junior Rank in their Regiments."

The Duke's prejudices were stronger than his facts. The statement, not very grammatically expressed, that "the practice of smoking" was "itself a species of intoxication" was absurd enough; but the allegation, introduced by a question-begging "undoubtedly," that smoking occasioned drinking was directly contrary to fact. It was the introduction of after-dinner smoking that largely helped to kill the bad old practice of continued after-dinner drinking.

Perhaps the best reflection of and comment upon the attitude of society towards smoking is to be found in the ironical, satirical pages of Thackeray. Let the reader turn to the confessions of George Fitz-Boodle Esq.--the "Fitz-Boodle Papers" first appeared in Fraser's Magazine for 1842--and he will find how smoking was regarded at that date, and what Thackeray, speaking through the puppet Fitz-Boodle, thought of it. George starts by saying: "I am not, in the first place, what is called a ladies' man, having contracted an irrepressible habit of smoking after dinner, which has obliged me to give up a great deal of the dear creatures' society; nor can I go much to country-houses for the same reason." The ladies had a keen scent for the abominable odour of tobacco, and distrusted the men who smoked. Here is Fitz-Boodle's, or Thackeray's, comment on it--"What is this smoking that it should be considered a crime? I believe in my heart that women are jealous of it, as of a rival. They speak of it as of some secret awful vice that seizes upon a man, and makes him a pariah from genteel society. I would lay a guinea that many a lady who has just been kind enough to read the above lines lays down the book, after this confession of mine that I am a smoker, and says, 'Oh, the vulgar wretch!' and passes on to something else." He goes on to prophesy--and for once the "most gratuitous of follies" has been justified by the event--that tobacco will conquer. "Look over the wide world," he says to the ladies, "and see that your adversary has overcome it. Germany has been puffing for three score years; France smokes to a man. Do you think you can keep the enemy out of England? Psha! look at his progress. Ask the club-houses, Have they smoking-rooms, or not? Are they not obliged to yield to the general want of the age, in spite of the resistance of the old women on the committees? I, for my part, do not despair to see a bishop lolling out of the 'Athenaeum' with a cheroot in his mouth, or, at any rate, a pipe stuck in his shovel-hat."

The flight of fancy in the last sentence has hardly yet been fulfilled; but I saw, many years ago, a distinguished man of letters, the late Mr. Francis Turner Palgrave, of "Golden Treasury" fame, who was an inveterate smoker, sitting on one of the cane benches by the door of the Athenaeum Club, smoking a short clay pipe.

Thackeray does not appear to have realized that tobacco was not invading England for the first, but for the second time, nor did he foresee that the ladies, to whom he addressed his impassioned defence of smoking, would not only submit to the conqueror but would themselves be found among his joyous devotees.

George Fitz-Boodle recounts how, as a boy, he was flogged for smoking, and how, at Oxford, smoking among other villainies led to his rustication. Later his tobacco, combined with insolence to his tobacco-hating colonel, conducted him out of the army into the retirement of civil life; and so on and so on. There is, of course, an element of exaggeration in all this; but Mr. Fitz-Boodle's experiences and reflections throw much light on the social history of smoking in the early decades of the nineteenth century. Mr. Harry Furniss, in the preface to his edition of Thackeray, has an admirably terse and pertinent paragraph on this aspect of the "Fitz-Boodle Papers." He says--"No gentleman in those days was seen smoking even a 'weed' in the streets. Cigarettes were practically unheard of in England, and outside one's private smoking-room pipes were tabooed. Men in Society slunk into their smoking-rooms, or, when there was no smoking-room, into the kitchen or servants' hall, after the domestics had retired. A smoking-jacket was worn in the place of their ordinary evening coat, and their well-oiled, massive head of hair was protected by a gorgeously decorated smoking-cap. Thus the odour of tobacco was not brought into the drawing-room."

The fear of the odour of tobacco-smoke was extraordinary. Mr. J.C. Buckmaster in his reminiscences describes the famous debating society at Cogers' Hall, and says that "after one night at the Cogers' it took three days on a common to purify your clothes" from the smoke. The journalists and Bohemians who met at the Cogers were above (or below) the dictates of fashion, and smoking was always a feature of their gatherings. The "yard of clay" is provided gratis for members, and it is to its almost universal use, says Mr. Peter Rayleigh, in his book on "The Cogers and Fleet Street," "that Cogers owe their existence in the present quarters. Once upon a time the Cogers 'swarmed' to a well-appointed room, where carpets covered the floors, the chairs were upholstered, and the tables had finely polished marble tops. The hot pipes and smouldering matches stained the table tops and burnt the carpets, so that they had the option of abandoning either the pipe or the quarters. Old customs die hard with Cogers, and they stuck to their pipe.... The pipe is a feature in all illustrations of Cogerian meetings."

The influence of the Court was wholly against smoking. Both Queen Victoria and the Prince Consort detested it, so tobacco was taboo wherever the Court was. The late Lady Dorothy Nevill, who lived to see the new triumph of tobacco, said that she thought the greatest minor change in social habits which she had witnessed was that in the attitude assumed towards smoking, which, in her youth, "and even later, was, except in certain well-defined circumstances, regarded as little less than a heinous crime." Lady Dorothy remarked that "smoking-rooms in country houses were absolutely unknown"--but that was not quite correct as we shall see in the experiences of Professor von Holtzendorff, to be mentioned directly--and that "such gentlemen as wished to smoke after the ladies had gone to bed used, as a matter of course, to go either to the servants' hall or to the harness-room in the stables, where at night some sort of rough preparation was generally made for their accommodation.... Well do I remember the immense care which devotees of tobacco used to take, when sallying forth in the country to enjoy it, not to allow the faintest whiff of smoke to penetrate into the hall as they lit their cigars at the door."

In 1845 Dickens wrote: "I generally take a cigar after dinner when I'm alone." The reservation in the last three words may be noted. In the "Book of Snobs," Major Wellesley Ponto goes to smoke a cigar in the stables--Ponto had no smoking-room--with Lord Gules, who is described as a "very young, short, sandy-haired and tobacco-smoking nobleman, who cannot have left the nursery very long." Later, Ponto and Gules "resume smoking operations ... in the now vacant kitchen."

Even so late as 1861 the attitude towards smoking was still much the same in some quarters. In that year a German scholar, Professor Franz von Holtzendorff, paid a visit to a country gentleman's house in Gloucestershire--Hardwicke Court. Later he printed an account of his experiences, a translation of which was published in this country in 1878. When the professor arrived, his host, the first greeting over, at once pointed out to him a secluded apartment--the one which he thought it most important for a German to know, namely, the smoking-room. "According to his idea," continued the professor, "every German has three national characteristics, smoking, singing, and Sabbath-breaking; the first and only idea in which I found him led astray by an abstract theory." Later, his hostess, explaining to him the method and routine of life in an English country-house, said that the ladies retired about eleven, while the gentlemen finished their day's work in the smoking-room--the secluded apartment--or enjoyed a cigar at the billiard-table; but a smoke in the billiard-room was only allowed if that room was not near the drawing-room or in the hall close by. "You must have often been surprised," she continued, "that we English ladies have such an invincible repugnance to tobacco smoke, but there is no dispensation from our rule of abstinence, except in those rooms which my husband has already pointed out to you."

The professor, after luncheon, was pressed by the squire--"who, on any other occasion would never waste time in smoking, and only filled his short clay pipe at the end of his day's work"--to come to his smoking-room. As regards this room the professor drily remarked--"I thought I had noticed that even the key-hole was stopped up, in order to preserve the ladies' delicate nerves from every disagreeable sensation." After dinner, again, when the ladies had left the table, "the gentlemen passed the bottles of port, sherry, and claret, with the regularity of planets from hand to hand," but no one dreamed of smoking. That was reserved for the secluded apartment after the ladies had gone to bed. Neither host nor guest imagined what a revolution another generation or so would make in these social habits.

In the 'fifties the pipes smoked were mostly clays. There were the long clays or "churchwardens," to be smoked in hours of ease and leisure; and the short clays--"cutties"--which could be smoked while a man was at work. Milo, a tobacconist in the Strand, and Inderwick, whose shop was near Leicester Square, were famous for their pipes, which could be bought for 6d. apiece. A burlesque poem of 1853, in praise of an old black pipe, says:

> Think not of meerschaum is that bowl: away,
> Ye fond enthusiasts! it is common clay,
> By Milo stamped, perchance by Milo's hand,
> And for a tizzy purchased in the Strand.
>
> Famed are the clays of Inderwick, and fair
> The pipes of Fiolet from Saint Omer.

I am indebted for this quotation to a correspondent of Notes and Queries, September 27, 1913.

Another correspondent of the same journal, Colonel W.F. Prideaux, also replying to a query of mine, wrote: "Before briar-root pipes came into common use clay pipes were of necessity smoked by all classes. When I matriculated at Oxford at the Easter of 1858 ... University men used to be rather particular about the pipes they smoked. The finest were made in France, and the favourite brand was 'Fiolet, Saint Omer.' I do not know if this kind is still smoked, but it was made of a soft clay that easily coloured. In taverns, of course, the churchwarden--beloved of Carlyle and Tennyson--was usually smoked to the accompaniment of shandygaff. At Simpson's fish ordinary at Billingsgate these pipes were always placed on the table after dinner, together with screws of shag tobacco, and a smoking parliament moistened with hot or cold punch according to the season, was generally held during the following hour. Of course, in those days no one ever thought of smoking a pipe in the presence of ladies."

Colonel Harold Malet at the same time wrote--"When I was a cadet at Sandhurst in 1855-58, Milo's cutty pipes were quite the thing, and the selection by cadets of a good one out of a fresh consignment packed in sawdust was eagerly watched by the 'Johns.' Of course we were imitating our parents." It was no doubt these cutty pipes which are referred to in one of the sporting books of Robert Surtees as the "clay pipes of gentility."

In a private letter to me, which I am privileged to quote, Colonel Prideaux adds some further particulars as to the social attitude of early Victorian days towards tobacco--particulars which are the more valuable and interesting as being supplied from personal recollection of those now somewhat distant days. The Colonel writes: "When I was a young man people never thought of smoking in what house-agents call the 'reception-rooms,' the principal reason being that the occupation of these rooms was shared by ladies, and it was 'bad form' (not, by the way, a contemporary expression) to smoke while in the company of the fairer half of creation. Consequently, men had either to indulge in the practice out of doors, or else, as you say, sneak away to the kitchen when the servants had gone to bed, and puff up the chimney. It was only in large houses that a billiard room could be found, and even in a billiard room a pipe or cigar was taboo if ladies were present, while smoking-rooms could no more be found in middle-class houses than bath-rooms. Both cutties and churchwardens were smoked, but the latter of course were not adapted for persons engaged in active pursuits and were essentially of what I may call a sedentary nature. You could not even walk while holding a long churchwarden in your mouth, and consequently the short clay was most favoured by young men at Sandhurst and the Universities.... Labourers smoked short clays when out of doors, and churchwardens when they rested from their labours and took their ease in their inn in the evenings."

Mr. Furniss, in the paragraph quoted on a previous page, says: "No gentleman in those days was seen smoking even a 'weed' in the streets." The nearest approach to this seems to have been smoking on club steps. Thackeray, in the seventeenth chapter of the "Book of Snobs," speaks of dandies smoking their cigars upon the steps of "White's," most fashionable of clubs, and, in an earlier chapter, of young Ensign Famish lounging and smoking on the steps of the "Union Jack Club," with half a dozen other "young rakes of the fourth or fifth order." Two of Thackeray's own drawings in the "Book of Snobs"--in chapters three and nine--show men, one civil the other military, smoking cigars out of doors; but as these were no doubt arrant snobs, the drawings may be accepted as proof of Mr. Furniss's statement.

In this same book Thackeray says ironically--"Think of that den of abomination, which, I am told, has been established in some *clubs, called the* Smoking-Room." The satirist was very familiar with the smoking-room at the club he loved well-- the "Little G."--the Garrick. The original Garrick club-house was at 35 King Street, Covent Garden, where the club was founded in 1831. It had formerly been a quiet, old-fashioned family hotel, but apparently was not furnished with a smoking-room, for one of the first acts of the club, when they obtained possession of the house, was to build out over the "leads" a large and comfortable smoking-room. Shirley Brooks said that this room, which was reached by a long passage from the Strangers' Dining-room, "was not a cheerful apartment by daylight, and when empty, but which, at night and full, was thought the most cheerful apartment in Town." At other clubs of more fashion, perhaps, but certainly of less good-fellowship, smoking-rooms made their way more slowly. At White's, smoking was not allowed at all till 1845. The Alfred Club, founded in 1808, which Lord Byron described as pleasant--"a little too sober and literary, perhaps, but, on the whole, a decent resource on a rainy day," and which Sir William Fraser called "a sort of minor Athenaeum," owed its death in 1855, if report be true, to a dispute about smoking. One section of the members wished for an improved smoking-room--they called the existing room, which was at the top of the house--an "infamous hole"--while the more old-fashioned and more influential members objected to any improvement. The latter carried the day, but the consequent loss of members ruined the club, which soon after ceased to exist. This secession must have been subsequent to that of the bishops, of whom at one time many were members, but who left, it is said, because of the introduction of a billiard-table!

The growth of cigar-smoking was rapid. Mr. Steinmetz, in his book on "Tobacco," published in 1857, remarked that no way of using tobacco had made a more striking advance in England within the preceding twenty years than cigars. For a long time it had been confined in this country to the richer class of smokers, but when he wrote it was "in universal use." The wonder is that with so many men smoking cigars the old domestic and club restrictions, as pilloried in Thackeray's pages, were maintained so long. In 1853 Leech had an admirably drawn sketch in Punch of paterfamilias, in the absence of his wife, giving a little dinner. Beside him sits his small son, and on either side of the table sit two of his cronies. One has a cigar in his hand and is blowing a cloud of smoke, while the other is selecting a "weed." The host is just lighting his cigar as the maid enters with a tray of decanters and glasses, and with disgust written plainly on her face. The objectionable child beside him says--"Lor! Pa, are you going to smoke? My eye! won't you catch it when Ma comes home, for making the curtains smell!"

Another witness to the rapid development of cigar-smoking is Captain Gronow, the author of the well-known "Reminiscences." Gronow says that the famous surgeon, Sir Astley Cooper, on one occasion perceiving that he was fond of smoking, cautioned him against that habit, telling him that it would, sooner or later, be the cause of his death. This must have been before 1841, when Sir Astley died. Writing in the 'sixties Gronow said: "If Sir Astley were now alive he would find everybody with a cigar in his mouth: men smoke nowadays whilst they are occupied in working or hunting, riding in carriages, or otherwise employed"--which shows how the prejudice against outdoor smoking was then breaking down. "During the experience of a long life, however," continued Gronow, "I never knew but one person of whom it was said that smoking was the cause of his death: he was the son of an Irish earl, and an attache at our embassy in Paris. But, alas! I have known thousands who have been carried off owing to their love of the bottle."

Thackeray, as the satirist of the foolish social prejudices against smoking, was naturally an inveterate smoker himself. He died in 1863, and so hardly saw the beginning of a change in the attitude of society towards the pestilent weed; but he was one of the many men of letters and artists, who, despising the conventions of society, were largely instrumental in breaking down stupid restrictions, and in overcoming senseless prejudices, and were thus heralds of freedom. Charles Keene's attitude was that of many artists. He smoked a little Jacobean clay pipe in his "sky-parlour" overlooking the Strand, and did not care in the least what the world might think or not think about that or any other subject.

Those who smoked pipes at Cambridge continued to smoke pipes afterwards, whatever "society" might do. Spedding, who spent his life on the elucidation of Bacon, was one of the "Apostles," and he continued a pipe-lover to the end. In 1832 we hear of Tennyson being in London with him, and "smoking all the day."

Lady Ritchie, in "Tennyson and his Friends," says: "I can remember vaguely, on one occasion through a cloud of smoke, looking across a darkening room at the noble, grave head of the Poet Laureate. He was sitting with my Father in the twilight after some family meal in the old house in Kensington." Thackeray was a cigar-smoker, but Tennyson was a devotee of the pipe. It was on this occasion, as the poet himself reminded Thackeray's daughter, that while the novelist was speaking, Lady Ritchie's little sister "looked up suddenly from the book over which she had been absorbed, saying in her sweet childish voice, 'Papa, why do you not write books like 'Nicholas Nickleby'?'"

Tennyson wrote "In Memoriam" at Shawell Rectory, near Lutterworth, Leicestershire. The rector was a Mr. Elmhirst, a native of the poet's Lincolnshire village. The latest historian of Lutterworth says that "The great puffs of tobacco smoke with which he [Tennyson] mellowed his thoughts, proved insufferable to his host, and he was accordingly turned out into Mr. Elmhirst's workshop in the garden, which in consequence became the birthplace of one of the gems of English literature."

About 1842, when Tennyson often dined at the Old Cock (by Temple Bar) and at other taverns, the perfect dinner for his taste, says his son, was "a beef-steak, a potato, a cut of cheese, a pint of port, and afterwards a pipe (never a cigar)." When the Kingsleys paid the Tennysons a visit about 1859, Charles Kingsley, so the Laureate told his son, "talked as usual on all sorts of topics, and walked hard up and down the study for hours smoking furiously, and affirming that tobacco was the only thing that kept his nerves quiet." The late Laureate, Alfred Austin, once asked Tennyson, after reading a passage in Dorothy Wordsworth's "Journal" that William had gone to bed "very tired" with writing the "Prelude," if he had ever felt tired by writing poetry. "I think not," said the poet, "but tired with the accompaniment of too much smoking."

Kingsley's devotion to smoke seems to have surprised Tennyson, who was no light smoker himself. The most curious story illustrating Kingsley's love of tobacco is that told in the life of Archbishop Benson by his son, Mr. A.C. Benson. One day about the year 1860, the future archbishop was walking with the Rector of Eversley in a remote part of the parish, on a common, when Kingsley suddenly said--"I must smoke a pipe," and forthwith went to a furze-bush and felt about in it for a time. Presently he produced a clay churchwarden pipe, "which he lighted, and solemnly smoked as he walked, putting it when he had done into a hole among some tree roots, and telling my father that he had a cache of pipes in several places in the parish to meet the exigencies of a sudden desire for tobacco." If this story did not appear in the life of an archbishop, some scepticism on the part of the reader might be excused.

Carlyle, as every one knows, was a great smoker. The story is familiar--it may be true--that one evening he and Tennyson sat in solemn silence smoking for hours, one on each side of the fireplace, and that when the visitor rose to go, Carlyle, as he bade him good-night, said--"Man, Alfred, we hae had a graund nicht; come again soon."

Tennyson's own devotion to tobacco led, on at least one occasion, to a peculiar and somewhat questionable proceeding. Mr. W.M. Rossetti had a temporary acquaintance with the poet, and in the "Reminiscences" which he published in 1906, he told a curious anecdote concerning him which was new to print. Rossetti told, on the authority of Woolner, how, in the course of a trip with friends to Italy, tobacco such as Tennyson could smoke gave out at some particular city, whereupon the poet packed up his portmanteau and returned home, breaking up the party! The late Joseph Knight, who reviewed Rossetti's volumes in the *Athenaeum*, vouched for the truth of this relation, which he had heard, not only from Woolner, but also from Tennyson's brother Septimus.

In more fashionable circles the mere possession of a pipe might be looked at askance. Robertson's comedy "Society" was produced in 1865, and in it, Tom Stylus, a somewhat Bohemian journalist, has the misfortune, in a fashionable ball-room, when pulling out his handkerchief to bring out his pipe with it from his pocket. The vulgar thing falls upon the floor, and Tom is ashamed to claim his property and so acknowledge his ownership of a pipe. He presently calls a footman, who comes with a tray and sugar-tongs, picks up the offending briar with the tongs, and carries it off "with an air of ineffable disgust."

Undergraduates, like men of letters, did not pay much attention to the conventional attitude of society towards tobacco, and pipes maintained their popularity in college rooms. Thackeray, in the "Book of Snobs," describes youths at a University wine-party as "drinking bad wines, telling bad stories, singing bad songs over and over again. Milk punch--smoking--ghastly headache--frightful spectacle of dessert-table next morning, and smell of tobacco." But the satirist is often tempted to be epigrammatic at the expense of accuracy, and this picture is at least too highly coloured. In the recently published memoir of "J"--John Willis Clark--some reminiscences of the late Registrary are included; and "J" does not recognize Thackeray's picture as quite true of the "wines" of his undergraduate day, i.e. about 1850. "They may," he says, "have 'told bad stories and sung bad songs,' as Thackeray says in his 'Book of Snobs.' I can only say that I never heard either the one or the other." But certainly there was noise, and there was smoke--plenty of it. "Conversation there was none," says "J," "only a noise. Then came smoke. In a short time the atmosphere became dense, the dessert and the wine came to an end, and it was chapel time (mercifully)." One story Clark tells of an extraordinary attempt to smoke. Referring to the compulsory "chapels," he says that as a rule everybody behaved with propriety, whether they regarded the attendance as irksome or otherwise. But, he admits, "'Iniquity Corner,' as the space at the east end on each side of the altar was called, may occasionally have effectually sheltered card-playing; but when a young snob went so far as to light a cigar there, he had the pleasure of finishing it in the country, for he was rusticated. It was on a cognate occasion in Jesus College, in which cobblers' wax played a prominent part, that Dr. Corrie dismissed the culprit, after a severe lecture, with these admirable words: 'Your conduct, sir, is what a Christian would call profane, and a gentleman vulgar.'"

At Oxford, in November 1859, the Vice-Chancellor and Proctors issued the following notice, which shows that an occasional outbreak of bad manners might happen on the Isis as on the Cam: "Whereas complaints have been made that some Undergraduate members of the University are in the habit of smoking at public entertainments, and otherwise creating annoyance, they are hereby cautioned against the repetition of such ungentlemanlike conduct."

There was plenty of smoking among undergraduates at Oxford in those days, as may be seen in such books as "The Adventures of Mr. Verdant Green," and Hughes's "Tom Brown at Oxford," both of which date from 1861. When Tom, after a reading-bout, thought of going out--"there was a wine party at one of his acquaintance's rooms; or he could go and smoke a cigar in the pool-room, or at any one of a dozen other places." Cigars were the fashionable form of smoke. When Tom offers his box to Captain Hardy, that worthy's son says: "You might as well give him a glass of absinthe. He is churchwarden at home, and can't smoke anything but a long clay," with which the old sailor was accordingly supplied.

A striking example of the attitude of the mid-nineteenth century days towards tobacco may be found in connexion with railways and railway travelling. In the early days of such travel there were no smoking compartments, and indeed smoking was "strictly forbidden" practically everywhere on railway premises. Relics of this time may still be seen in many stations and on many platforms in the shape of somewhat dingy placards announcing that smoking is strictly forbidden, and that the penalty is so much. Nowadays the incense from pipes and cigars and cigarettes curls freely round these obsolete notices and helps to make them still dingier. If you wanted to smoke when travelling you had either to contrive to get a compartment to yourself, or to arrange terms with your fellow-travellers. In a Punch *of 1855, Leech drew a railway-platform scene wherein figures one of those precocious youngsters of a type he loved to draw. A railway porter says to his mate, as the two gaze at the back of this small swell, with his cane and top-hat, "What does he say, Bill?" "Why, he says he must have a compartment to hisself, because he can't get on without his smoke!" Another drawing in a* Punch *of 1861 points the same moral. It represents an elderly "party" and a "fast Etonian" seated side by side in a first-class compartment. The latter has a cigar in one hand and with the other offers coins to his neighbour; the explanation is as follows:* "Old Party. *Really, sir,--I am the manager of the line, sir--I must inform you that if you persist in smoking, you will be fined forty shillings, sir.* Fast Etonian. Well, old boy, I must have my smoke; so you may as well take your forty shillings now!"

Tobacco was always popular in the army; and even the strongest of anti-tobacconists would have felt that there was at least something, if not much, to be said for the abused weed, when in times of campaigning suffering it played so beneficent a part in soothing and comforting weary and wounded men. The period covered by this chapter included both the Crimean War and the Indian Mutiny, and every one knows how the soldiers in the Crimea and in India alike craved for tobacco as for one of the greatest of luxuries, and how even an occasional smoke cheered and encouraged and sustained suffering humanity. The late Dr. Norman Kerr, who was no friend to ordinary, everyday smoking, wrote: "There are occasions, such as in the trenches during military operations, when worn out with exposure and fatigue, or when exhausted by slow starvation with no food in prospect, when a pipe or cigar will be a welcome and valuable friend in need, resting the weary limbs, cheering the fainting heart, allaying the gnawing hunger of the empty stomach."

Sir G.W. Forrest, in his book on "The Indian Mutiny," tells how at the siege of Lucknow, as the month of August advanced, "the tea and sugar, except a small store kept for invalids, were exhausted. The tobacco also was gone, and Europeans and natives suffered greatly from the want of it. The soldiers yearned for a pipe after a hard day's work, and smoked dry leaves as the only substitute they could obtain." Mr. L.E.R. Rees in his diary of the same siege noted--"I have given up smoking tobacco, and have taken to tea-leaves and neem-leaves, and guava fruit-leaves instead, which the poor soldiers are also constantly using." The neem-tree is better known, perhaps, as the margosa. It yields a bitter oil, and is supposed to possess febrifugal properties.

Among the general mass of the population in the early Victorian period, smoking, though certainly not so all-prevailing as now, was yet very common. It is highly probable that one of the things which led to the great increase in pipe-smoking which took place from this time onwards was the introduction of the briar pipe.

The earliest example of the use of a wooden pipe I have met with is dated 1765--but this was not in England. Many years ago the late Mr. A.J. Munby pointed out that Smollett, in one of his letters dated March 18, 1765, giving an account of his journey from Nice to Turin, describes how he ascended "the mountain Brovis," and on the top thereof met a Quixotic figure, whom he thus pictures: "He was very tall, meagre, and yellow, with a long hooked nose and twinkling eyes. His head was cased in a woollen nightcap, over which he wore a flapped hat; he had a silk handkerchief about his neck, and his mouth was furnished with a short wooden pipe, from which he discharged wreathing clouds of tobacco-smoke." This scarecrow turned out to be an Italian marquis; and no doubt the singularity of his smoking apparatus was of a piece with the singularity of his attire.

Mr. Munby, after this reference to Smollett's adventure, proceeded to claim the honour of having helped to bring the use of wooden pipes into England. In the year 1853 he wrote, "meerschaums and clays were the rule at both the English universities and in all shops throughout the land, and the art of making pipes of wood was either obsolete [it had never been introduced] or wholly in futuro. But a college friend of mine, a Norfolk squire, possessed a gardener who was of an inventive turn, though he was not a Scotchman. This man conceived and wrought out the idea of making pipes of willow-wood, cutting the bowl out of a thick stem, and the tube out of a thinner one growing from the bowl, so that the whole pipe was in one piece. Willow-wood is too soft, so that the pipes did not last long; but they were a valuable discovery, and the young squire's friends bought them eagerly at eighteenpence apiece."

This experiment in the direction of wooden pipes was interesting, and deserves to be remembered; but it was not long before the briar was introduced and carried everything before it.

It was about 1859 that the use of the root of the White Heath (Erica arborea), a native of the South of France, Corsica, and some other localities, for the purpose of making tobacco-pipes was introduced into this country. The word "brier" or "briar" has no connexion whatever with the prickly, thorny briar which bears the lovely wild rose. It is derived from the French bruyere, heath--the root of the White Heath being the material known as "briar" or "brier," and at first as "bruyer." The Oxford Dictionary quotes an advertisement from the Tobacco Trade Review of so recent a date as February 8, 1868, of a "Heath Pipe: in Bruyer Wood." The briar pipe not only soon drove the clay largely out of use, but immensely increased the number of pipe-smokers. Bulwer Lytton may not have known the briar, but he wrote enthusiastically of the pipe. Every smoker knows the glowing tribute he paid to it in his "Night and Morning," which appeared in 1841. It is terser and more to the point than most panegyrics: "A pipe! It is a great soother, a pleasant comforter. Blue devils fly before its honest breath. It ripens the brain, it opens the heart; and the man who smokes thinks like a sage and acts like a Samaritan."

XI
LATER VICTORIAN DAYS

When life was all a summer day,
And I was under twenty,
Three loves were scattered in my way--
And three at once are plenty.
 Three hearts, if offered with a grace,
One thinks not of refusing.
The task in this especial case
Was only that of choosing.
I knew not which to make my pet--
My pipe, cigar, or cigarette.
       HENRY S. LEIGH.

The social history of smoking in later Victorian days is marked by the triumph of the cigarette. The introduction of the cigar, as we have seen, brought about the revival of smoking, from the point of view of fashion, in the early decades of the nineteenth century; and the coming of the cigarette completed what the cigar had begun.

The earliest references for the word "cigarette" in the Oxford Dictionary are dated 1842 and 1843, but both refer to the smoking of cigarettes abroad--in France and Italy. The 1843 quotation is from a book by Mrs. Romer, in which she says--"The beggars in the streets have paper cigars (called cigarettes) in their mouths." The wording here would seem to show that cigarettes were not then familiar to English people.

Laurence Oliphant, who was both a man of letters and a man of fashion, is generally credited with the introduction into English society of the cigarette; but it is difficult to suggest even an approximate date. Writing from Boulogne to W.H. Wills in September 1854, Dickens says, "I have nearly exhausted the cigarettes I brought here," and proceeds to give directions for some to be sent to him from London. This is the earliest reference I have found to cigarette-smoking in England; but it is possible that by "cigarettes" Dickens meant not what we now know as such, but simply small cigars. Mr. H.M. Hyndman, in his "Record of an Adventurous Life," says that when he was living as a pupil, about the year 1860, with the Rector of Oxburgh, his fellow-pupils included "Edward Abbott of Salonica, who, poor fellow, was battered to pieces by the Turks with iron staves torn from palings at the beginning of the Turco-Servian War. Cigarette-smoking, now so popular, was then almost unknown, and Abbott, who always smoked the finest Turkish tobacco which he rolled up into cigarettes for himself, was the first devotee of this habit I encountered."

Fairholt, in his book on "Tobacco," which was published in 1859, mentions cigarettes as being smoked in Spain and South and Central America, but makes no reference to their use in this country.

The late Lady Dorothy Nevill said that although cigarettes are a modern invention, she believed that they already existed in a slightly different form at the beginning of the nineteenth century, "when old Peninsular officers used to smoke tobacco rolled up tight in a piece of paper. They called this a papelito, and I fancy it was much the same thing as a cigarette." But if this were so, the habit must have died out long before the cigarette, as we now know it, came into vogue.

It may fairly be concluded, I think, that although about 1860 there may have been an occasional cigarette-smoker in England, like the Edward Abbott of Mr. Hyndman's reminiscences, yet it was not until a little later date that the small paper-enclosed rolls of tobacco became at all common among Englishmen; and it is quite likely that the credit (or discredit, as the reader pleases) of bringing them into general, and especially into fashionable, use, has been rightly given to Laurence Oliphant.

Cigarettes were perhaps in fashion in 1870. In "Puck," which was published in that year, Ouida--who is hardly an unimpeachable authority on the ways and customs of fashionable folk, though she loved to paint fancy pictures of their sayings and doings--pictures the Row: "the most fashionable lounge you have, but it is a Republic for all that." There, she says, "could Bill Jacobs lean against a rail, with a clay-pipe in his mouth, and a terrier under his arm, close beside the Earl of Guil-liadene, with his cigarette and his eye-glass, and his Poole-cut habiliments."

Thirty years or more ago the late Andrew Lang wrote an article entitled "Enchanted Cigarettes," which began--"To dream our literary projects, Balzac says, is like 'smoking enchanted cigarettes,' but when we try to tackle our projects, to make them real, the enchantment disappears--we have to till the soil, to sow the weed, to gather the leaves, and then the cigarettes must be manufactured, while there may be no market for them after all. Probably most people have enjoyed the fragrance of these cigarettes and have brooded over much which they will never put on paper. Here are some of 'the ashes of the weeds of my delight'--memories of romances whereof no single line is written, or is likely to be written." What Balzac said in his "La Cousine Bette" was--"Penser, rever, concevoir de belles oeuvres est une occupation delicieuse. C'est fumer des cigares enchantes, c'est mener la vie de la courtisane occupee a sa fantaisie." Balzac's cigars became cigarettes in Lang's fantasy. The French novelist seems to have been one of those who praised tobacco without using it much himself. In his "Illusions Perdues" Carlos Herrera, who was Vautrin, says to Lucien, whom he meets on the point of suicide: "Dieu nous a donne le tabac pour endormir nos passions et nos douleurs." M.A. Le Breton, however, in his book on Balzac--"L'Homme et L'OEuvre"--says: "Il ne se soutient qu'a force de cafe," though he would sit working at his desk for twenty-five hours running.

About the time that Lang's article was written, Sir F.C. Burnand's burlesque, "Bluebeard" was produced at the Gaiety Theatre. In those days a certain type of young man, since known by many names, including the present day "nut," was called a "masher"; and Burnand's burlesque included a duet with the refrain:

We are mashers, we are,
As we smoke our cigar
And crawl along, never too quick;
We are mashers, you bet,
With the light cigarette
And the quite irreproachable stick.

Nowadays the cigarette is in such universal use, that it would be impossible thus to associate it with any particular type of man, sane or inane.

The late Bishop Mandell Creighton, of London, was an incessant smoker of cigarettes. Mr. Herbert Paul, in his paper on the Bishop, says that those who went to see him at Fulham on a Sunday afternoon always found him, if they found him at all, "leisurely, chatty, hospitable, and apparently without a care in the world. There was the family tea-table, and there were the eternal cigarettes. The Bishop must have paid a fortune in tobacco-duty." There is a side view of another tobacco-lover in the "Note-Books" of Samuel Butler, the author of "Erewhon." Creighton, after reading Butler's "Alps and Sanctuaries" had asked the author to come and see him. Butler was in doubt whether or not to go, and consulted his clerk, Alfred, on the matter. That wise counsellor asked to look at the Bishop's letter, and then said: "I see, sir, there is a crumb of tobacco in it; I think you can go."

Apart from cigarette-smoking, however, the use of tobacco grew steadily during the later Victorian period. In "Mr. Punch's Pocket-Book" for 1878 there was a burlesque dialogue between uncle and nephew entitled "Cupid and 'Baccy." The uncle thinks the younger men smoke too much, and declares that tobacco "has destroyed the susceptibility, which in my time made youngsters fall in love, as they often did, with a girl without a penny. No fellow can fall in love when he has continually a pipe in his mouth; and if he ever feels inclined to when it would be imprudent, why he lights his pipe, and very soon smokes the idea of such folly out of his head. Not so when I was of your age. Besides a few old farmers, churchwardens, and overseers, and such, nobody then ever smoked but labourers and the lower orders--cads as you now say. Smoking was thought vulgar. Young men never smoked at all. To smoke in the presence of a lady was an inconceivable outrage; yet now I see you and your friends walking alongside of one another's sisters, smoking a short pipe down the street." "The girls like it," says Nepos. "In my time," replies Avunculus, "young ladies would have fainted at the bare suggestion of such an enormity." The dialogue ends as follows:

"NEPOS (producing short clay). See here, Uncle. This pipe is almost coloured. How long do you think I have had it?

"AVUNCULUS. Can't imagine.

"NEPOS. Only three weeks.

"AVUNCULUS. Good boy!"

In the same "Pocket-Book" one of the ideals of a wife by a bachelor is--"To approve of smoking all over the house"; while one of the ideals of a husband by a spinster is--"Not to smoke, or use a latch-key." Mr. Punch's prelections, of course, are not to be taken too seriously. They all necessarily have the exaggeration of caricature; but at the same time they are all significant, and for the social historian are invaluable.

Tobacco-smoking was advancing victoriously all along the line. Absurd old conventions and ridiculous restrictions had to give way or were broken through in every direction. The compartments for smokers on railway trains, at first provided sparsely and grudgingly, became more and more numerous. The practice of smoking out of doors, which the early Victorians held in particular abhorrence, became common--at least so far as cigars and cigarettes were concerned. Lady Dorothy Nevill, whose memory covered so large a part of the nineteenth century, said, in the "Leaves" from her note-book which was published in 1907, that to smoke in Hyde Park, even up to comparatively recent years, was looked upon as absolutely unpardonable; while smoking anywhere with a lady would, in the earlier days, have been classed as an almost disgraceful social crime. The first gentleman of whom Lady Dorothy heard as having been seen smoking a cigar in the Park was the Duke of Sutherland, and the lady who told her spoke of it as if she had been present at an earthquake! Pipes were (and are) still looked at askance in many places where the smoking of cigars and cigarettes is freely allowed, and fashion frowned on the pipe in street or Park.

Of course, what one might do in the country and what one might do in town were two quite different things. The following story was told nearly twenty years ago of the late Duke of Devonshire. An American tourist began talking one day to a quiet-looking man who was smoking outside an inn on the Chatsworth estate, and, taking the man for the inn-keeper, expressed his admiration of the Duke of Devonshire's domain. "Quite a place, isn't it?" said the American. "Yes, a pleasant place enough," returned the Englishman. "The fellow who owns it must be worth a mint of money," said the American, through his cigar-smoke. "Yes, he's comfortably off," agreed the other. "I wonder if I could get a look at the old chap," said the stranger, after a short silence; "I should like to see what sort of a bird he is." Puff, puff, went the English cigar, and then said the English voice, trying hard to control itself: "If you"--puff--"look hard"--puff, puff--"in this direction, you"--puff, puff--"can tell in a minute." "You, you!" faltered the American, getting up, "why, I thought you were the landlord!" "Well, so I am," said the Duke, "though I don't perform the duties." "I stay here," he added, with a twinkle in his eye, "to be looked at."

Among the chief strongholds of the old ideas and prejudices were some of the clubs. At the Athenaeum the only smoking-room used to be a combined billiard- and smoking-room in the basement. It was but a few years ago that an attic story was added to the building, and smokers can now reach more comfortable quarters by means of a lift put in when the alterations were made in 1900. This new smoking-room is a very handsome, largely book-lined apartment. At the end of the room is a beautiful marble mantelpiece of late eighteenth century Italian work. At White's even cigars had not been allowed at all until 1845; and when, in 1866, some of the younger members wished to be allowed to smoke in the drawing-room, there was much perturbation, the older members bitterly opposing the proposal. "A general meeting was held to decide the question," says Mr. Ralph Nevill, in his "London Clubs," "when a number of old gentlemen who had not been seen in the club for years made their appearance, stoutly determined to resist the proposed desecration. 'Where do all these old fossils come from?' inquired a member. 'From Kensal Green,' was Mr. Alfred Montgomery's reply. 'Their hearses, I understand, are waiting to take them back there.'" The motion for the extension of the facilities for smoking was defeated by a majority of twenty-three votes, and as an indirect result the Marlborough Club was founded. The late King Edward, at that time Prince of Wales, is said to have sympathized strongly with the defeated minority at White's, and to have interested himself in the foundation of the Marlborough; where, "for the first time in the history of West End Clubland, smoking, except in the dining-room, was everywhere allowed." By "smoking" is no doubt here meant everything but pipes, which were not considered gentlemanly even at the Garrick Club at the beginning of the present century. The late Duc d'Aumale was a social pioneer in pipe-smoking. His caricature in "Vanity Fair" represents him with a pipe in his mouth, although he is wearing an opera-hat, black frock-coat buttoned up, and a cloak.

By the end of the nineteenth century the snuff-box which once upon a time stood upon the mantelpiece of every club, had disappeared. The habit of snuffing had long been falling into desuetude. The cigar dealt the snuff-box its death-blow and the cigarette was chief mourner at its funeral.

As in other periods, men of letters and artists ignored the social prejudices and conventions about tobacco, and laughed at the artificial distinctions drawn between cigars and pipes. It is said that the late Sir John Millais smoked a clay pipe in his carriage when he was part of the first Jubilee procession of Queen Victoria--a performance, if it took place, which would certainly have horrified her tobacco-hating Majesty. Tennyson and his friends smoked their pipes as they had always done--and old-fashioned clay pipes too. Sir Norman Lockyer, referring to a period about 1867, mentions Monday evenings in his house which were given up to friends "who came in, sans ceremonie, to talk and smoke. Clays from Broseley, including 'churchwardens' and some of larger size (Frank Buckland's held an ounce of tobacco) were provided, and the confirmed smokers (Tennyson, an occasional visitor, being one of them) kept their pipes, on which the name was written, in a rack for future symposia."

Of the other great Victorian poets Morris was a pipe-smoker, and so was Rossetti. Browning also smoked, but not, I think, a pipe. Swinburne, on the other hand, detested tobacco, and expressed himself on the subject with characteristic extravagance and vehemence--"James I was a knave, a tyrant, a fool, a liar, a coward. But I love him, I worship him, because he slit the throat of that blackguard Raleigh who invented this filthy smoking!" Professor Blackie, in a letter to his wife, remarked: "The first thing I said on entering the public room was--'What a delightful thing the smell of tobacco is, in a warm room on a wet night!' ... I gave my opinion with great decision that tobacco, whisky and all such stimulants or sedatives, had their foundation in nature, could not be abolished, or rather should not, and must be content with the check of a wise regulation. Even pious ladies were fond of tea, which, taken in excess, was worse for the nerves than a glass of sherry."

One of the most distinguished of Victorian men of letters, John Ruskin, was a great hater of tobacco. Notwithstanding this, he sent Carlyle--an inveterate smoker--a box of cigars in February 1865. In his letter of acknowledgment Carlyle wrote--"Dear Ruskin, you have sent me a magnificent Box of Cigars; for which what can I say in answer? It makes me both sad and glad. Ay de mi

'We are such stuff,
Gone with a puff--
Then think, and smoke Tobacco!'"

In the later years of his life, spent at Brantwood, Ruskin's guests found that smoking was not allowed even after dinner.

Another and greater Victorian, Gladstone, was also a non-smoker. He is said, however, on one occasion, when King Edward as Prince of Wales dined with him in Downing Street, to have toyed with a cigarette out of courtesy to his illustrious guest.

It was in the latter years of his life that Tennyson told Sir William Harcourt one day that his morning pipe after breakfast was the best in the day--an opinion, by the way, to which many less distinguished smokers would subscribe--when Sir William laughingly replied, "The earliest pipe of half-awakened bards."

The companion burlesque line, "The earliest pipe of half-awakened birdseye" appears, with one from Homer and one from Virgil, at the head of Arthur Sidgwick's poem in Greek Iambics, "+TO BAKCHO+," in "Echoes from the Oxford Magazine," 1890.

Sidgwick's praise of tobacco, classically draped in Greek verse, occasionally of the macaronic order, is delightful. He hails the pipe as the work of Pan, and the divine smoke as the best and most fragrant of gifts--healer of sorrow, companion in joy, rest for the toilers, drink for the thirsty, warmth for the cold, coolness in the heat, and a cheap feast for those who waste away through hunger. How is it, he says, that through so many ages men, who have need of thee, have not seen thy nature? Often, he continues--the verses may be roughly translated--often, when I am in Alpine solitudes, tied in a chain to a few companions, clinging to the rope, while barbarians lead the way, carrying in my hands an ice-axe (+krustalloplega chersin axinen pheron+), and breathless crawling up the snow-covered plain--then, when groaning I reach the summit (either pulled up or on foot), how have I rested, on my back on the rocks, charming my soul with thy divine clouds! He goes on in burlesque strain to speak of the joys of tobacco when he lies in idleness by the streams in breathless summer, comforted by a bath just taken, or when in the middle of the night he is worn out by revising endless exercises, underlining the mistakes in red and allotting marks, or weighed down by the wise men of old--Thucydides, Sophocles, Euripides, the ideas of Plato, wiles of Pindar, fearfully corrupt strophe of chorus, wondrous guesses of Teutons and fancies of philologists, when men swoon in the inexplicable wanderings of the endless examination of Homer, when the brain reels among such toil--then he hails the pipe, help of mortals, and hastens to kindle sacrifices at its altars and rejoices as he tastes its smoke. Let some one, he exclaims, bring Bryant and May's fire, which strikes a light only if rubbed on the box--

+enenkato tis pur bruantomaikon+
(+kausai d' adunaton me ouchi pros kiste tribeu+)

and taking the best and blackest bowl, and putting on Persian slippers, sitting on the softest couch, I will light my pipe, with my feet on the hearth, and I will cast aside all mortal care!

Nor must the delightful verses by "J.K.S." be forgotten, in which the author of "Lapsus Calami" sings of the "Grand Old Pipe"--

And I'm smoking a pipe which is fashioned
Like the face of the Grand Old Man;

and the quaint similarity or comparison between the pipe and Gladstone, the "Grand Old Man" when "Lapsus Calami" appeared in 1888, is maintained throughout--

Grows he black in his face with his labours?
Well, so does my Grand Old Pipe.

For the sake of its excellent savour,
For the many sweet smokes of the past
My pipe keeps its hold on my favour,
Tho' now it is blackening fast.

But although many pipes were smoked at the Universities, there were occasionally to be found odd survivals of old prejudices. Dr. Shipley, in his recent memoir of John Willis Clark, the Cambridge Registrary, says that even in the 'seventies of the last century there was an elderly Don at Cambridge who once rebuked a Junior Fellow, who was smoking a pipe in the Wilderness, with the remark, "No Christian gentleman smokes a pipe, or if he does he smokes a cigar." The perpetrator of this bull was the same parson who married late in life, and returning to his church after a honeymoon of six weeks, publicly thanked God "for three weeks of unalloyed connubial bliss."

XII
SMOKING IN THE TWENTIETH CENTURY

Sweet when the morn is grey;
Sweet, when they've clear'd away
Lunch; and at close of day
Possibly sweetest.
      C.S. CALVERLEY.

Tobacco is once more triumphant. The cycle of three hundred years is complete. Since the early decades of the seventeenth century, smoking has never been so generally practised nor so smiled upon by fashion as it is at the present time. Men in their attitude towards tobacco have always been divisible into three classes--those who respected and followed and obeyed the conventions of society and the dictates of fashion, and smoked or did not smoke in accordance therewith; those who knew those conventions but disregarded them and smoked as and what they pleased; and those who neither knew nor cared whether such conventions existed, or what fashion might say, but smoked as and what, and when and where they pleased. At the present time the three classes tend to combine into one. There are, it is true, a few conventions and restrictions left; but they are not very strong, and will probably disappear one of these days. There is also, of course, and always has been, a fourth class of men, who for one reason or another, quite apart from what fashion may say or do, do not smoke at all.

Perhaps the most absurd and unmeaning of the restrictions that remain, is that which at certain times and in certain places admits the smoking of cigars and cigarettes and forbids the smoking of pipes. The idea appears to be that a pipe is vulgar. There are few restaurants now in which smoking is not allowed after dinner;

but the understanding is that cigars and cigarettes only shall be smoked. In some places of resort there are notices exhibited which specifically prohibit the smoking of pipes. Why? At a smoking concert where few pipes are smoked, anyone looking

> Athwart the smoke of burning weeds

can at once realize how much greater is the volume of smoke from cigars and cigarettes than would result from the smoking of a like number of pipes. It cannot, therefore, be that pipes are barred because of a supposed greater effect upon the atmosphere of the room. The only conclusion the observer can come to is, that the fashionable attitude towards pipes is one of the last relics of the old social attitude- -the attitude of Georgian and Early Victorian days--towards smoking of any kind. The cigar and the cigarette were first introduced among the upper classes of society, and their use has spread downward. They have broken down many barriers, and in many places, and under many and divers conditions, the pipe has followed trium- phantly in their wake; but the last ditch of the old prejudice has been found in the convention, which, in certain places and at certain times, admits the cigar and ciga- rette of fashionable origin, but bars the entry of the plebeian pipe--the pipe which for two centuries was practically the only mode of smoking used or known.

An article which appeared in the Morning Post of February 20, 1913, may be regarded as a sign of the times. It was entitled "A Plea for the Pipe: By one who Smokes it." "I should like," said the writer, "pipe-men of all degrees to ask them- selves whether the time has not really arrived to enter a protest against the conven- tion which forces the pipe into a position of inferiority, and exalts to a pinnacle of undeserved pre-eminence the cigar, and still more the cigarette ... why should it be considered a mark of vulgarity, of plebeianism, to inhale tobacco-smoke through the stem of a briar, and the hall-mark of good breeding to finger a cigar or dally with that triviality and travesty of the adoration of My Lady Nicotine--a cigarette?" To these questions there can be but one answer: and the future, there can be little doubt, will emphasize that answer, and abolish the unmeaning convention.

The prejudice against the pipe is not confined to places of indoor resort. There are many men who smoke pipes within doors, who yet would not care to be seen in London smoking a pipe in the street, or in the park. In some circumstances this is quite intelligible. The writer of the Morning Post article remarked with much force and good sense that "Apart from social environment, there is a certain affinity between pipes and clothes. It is considered 'bad form' for a man in a frock-coat and silk hat to be seen smoking a pipe in the streets. If you are wearing a bowler hat and a lounge suit you may walk along with a briar protruding from your lips, and no one will think ill of you. If you are a son of toil garbed in your habit as you work, there is nothing incongruous in a well-seasoned clay or a 'nose-warmer,' which, for convenience, you carry upside down. Not so very long ago it was considered unseemly to smoke a pipe at all in the street unless you belonged to the humbler orders, who inhale their nicotine through the stem of a clay and expectorate with a greater sense of freedom than of responsibility."

At a few clubs there are still some curious and rather unmeaning restrictions. A particularly absurd rule that maintains its ground here and there, is that which forbids smoking in the library of a club. What more appropriate place could there be for the thoughtful consumption of tobacco than among the books? But after due allowance has been made for a few minor restrictions of this kind, the fact remains that smoking has triumphed socially all along the line in Clubland. We have travelled far from the days when a committee man could declare that "No Gentleman smoked," to the time when, for example, the large smoking-room at Brooks's is one of the finest rooms in one of the most famous and exclusive of clubs. This splendid room in the eighteenth-century days of gambling was the "Grand Subscription Room"--the gambling room of Georgian times. It still retains two of the old gaming tables. Now this magnificent apartment, with its splendid barrelled ceiling, which a well-known architectural writer, Mr. Stanley C. Ramsey, A.R.I.B.A., describes as "probably the finest room of its kind in London," is the temple of Saint Nicotine. The strangers' smoking-room in the same club, formerly the dining-room, is another beautiful and delightfully decorated apartment. Similar transformations have been witnessed in other clubs.

Barry's original plan for the Travellers' Club, erected in 1832, shows no smoking-room on the ground floor. It was probably some inconvenient apartment of no account. The early "Travellers" did smoke, for Theodore Hook, satirizing them and the club rule that no person was eligible as a member who had not travelled out of the British Islands to a distance of at least 500 miles from London in a direct line, wrote:

The travellers are in Pall Mall, and smoke cigars so
cosily,
And dream they climb the highest Alps, or rove the
plains of Moselai,
The world for them has nothing new, they have explored
all parts of it;
And now they are club-footed! and they sit and look at
charts of it.

The present-day smoking-room at the Travellers' is a noble apartment, which
was originally the coffee-room. It occupies the whole of the ground-floor front to
the gardens of Carlton House Terrace, and is divided into three bays by the projec-
tion of square piers.

Another sign of the complete change which has come over the attitude of most
folk towards tobacco is to be seen in the permission of smoking at meetings of committees and councils, where not so long ago such an indulgence would have been
regarded as an outrage. Many of the committees of municipal councils and other
public bodies now permit smoking while business is proceeding. It has even become
usual for members of the House of Commons to smoke in committee rooms when
the sitting is private; and cigars and cigarettes and pipes are now lighted in the lobby the moment that the House has risen. A very thin line thus separates the legisla-
tive chamber itself from the conquering weed. A further step forward (or backward,
according to each reader's judgment) was taken on July 21, 1913, when smoking
was allowed at the sitting of the Standing Committee on Scottish Bills--one of the
committees which does not conduct its business in private. On this occasion, after
the luncheon interval, two members entered the committee room smoking, one a
cigarette the other a cigar. The former was soon finished; but the latter continued
to shed its fragrance on the room. Naturally the chairman, Mr. Arthur Henderson,
was appealed to. He gave a diplomatic reply. It had been held, he said, by two chair-
men that smoking was not in order at the public sessions of a Standing Committee;
and, of course, if his ruling were formally asked he would be bound to follow prec-
edent. He said this with a suavity and a smile which disarmed any possible objector.
Nobody raised the formal point of order; so other members "lighted up," and the

proceedings went on peacefully to the appointed hour of closing.

Yet another sign of the times was the permission given not so very long ago to the drivers of taxi-cabs to smoke while driving fares--a development regarding which there may well be two opinions.

The number of cigarette-smokers nowadays is legion; but to a very large number of "tobacconists" (in the old sense of the word) a pipe remains the most satisfactory of "smokes." A cigar or a cigarette is--and it is not; the pipe renders its service again and again and yet remains--a steadfast companion. "Over a pipe" is a phrase of more meaning than "over a cigarette." Discussions are best conducted over a pipe. No one can get too excited or over-heated in argument, no one can neglect the observance of the amenities of conversation, who talks thoughtfully between the pulls at his pipe, who has to pause now and again to refill, to strike a light, to knock out the ashes, or to perform one of those numberless little acts of devotion at the shrine of St. Nicotine, which fill up the pauses and conduce to reflection. The Indians were wise in their generation when they made the circulation of the pipe an essential part of their pow-wows. A conference founded on the mutual consumption of tobacco was likely, not, as the frivolous would say, to end in smoke, but to lead to solid and lasting results. "The fact is, squire," said Sam Slick, "the moment a man takes a pipe he becomes a philosopher." The pipe, says Thackeray, "draws wisdom from the lips of the philosopher, and shuts up the mouth of the foolish; it generates a style of conversation, contemplative, thoughtful, benevolent and unaffected.... May I die if I abuse that kindly weed which has given me so much pleasure."

And what more fitting emblem of peace could be chosen than the calumet, the proffered pipe? Tobacco, whatever its enemies may have said, or may yet say, is the friend of peace, the foe of strife, and the promoter of geniality and good fellowship. Mrs. Battle, whose serious energies were all given to the great game of whist, unbent her mind, we are told, over a book. Most men unbend over a pipe, even if the book is an accompaniment.

To the solitary man the well-seasoned tube is an invaluable companion. If he happen, once in a way, to have nothing special to do and plenty of time in which to do it, he naturally fills his pipe as he draws the easy-chair on to the hearthrug, and knows not that he is lonely. If he have a difficult problem to solve, he just as naturally attacks it over a pipe. It is true that as the smoke-wreaths ring themselves above his head, his mind may wander off into devious paths of reverie, and the problem be utterly forgotten. Well, that is, at least, something for which to be grateful, for the paths of reverie are the paths of pleasantness and peace, and problems can usually afford to wait.

"Over a pipe!" Why the words bring up innumerable pleasant associations. The angler, having caught the coveted prize, refills his pipe, and with the satisfied sense of duty done, as the rings curl upward he reviews the struggle and glows again with victory. At the end of any day's occupation, especially one of pleasurable toil--whether it be shooting or hunting, or walking or what not--what can be pleasanter than to let the mind meander through the course of the day's proceedings over a pipe?

There is much wisdom in Robert Louis Stevenson's remarks in "Virginibus Puerisque"--"Lastly (and this is, perhaps, the golden rule), no woman should marry a teetotaller, or a man who does not smoke. It is not for nothing that this 'ignoble tabagie,' as Michelet calls it, spreads over all the world. Michelet rails against it because it renders you happy apart from thought or work; to provident women this will seem no evil influence in married life. Whatever keeps a man in the front garden, whatever checks wandering fancy and all inordinate ambition, whatever makes for lounging and contentment, makes just so surely for domestic happiness."

Nothing is more marked in the change in the social attitude towards tobacco than the revolution which has taken place in woman's view of smoking. The history of smoking by women is dealt with separately in the next chapter; but here it may be noted that most of the old intolerance of tobacco has disappeared. "To smoke in Hyde Park," said the late Lady Dorothy Nevill, in 1907, "even up to comparatively recent years, was looked upon as absolutely unpardonable, while smoking anywhere with a lady would have been classed as an almost disgraceful social crime."

Women do not nowadays shun the smell of smoke as they did in early Victorian days, as if it were the most dreadful of odours. They are tolerant of smoking in their presence, in public places, in restaurants--in fact, wherever men and women congregate--to a degree that would have horrified extremely their mothers and grandmothers. It is only within the last few years that visits to music-halls and theatres of varieties have been socially possible to ladies. Men go largely because they can smoke during the performance; women go largely because they have ceased to consider tobacco-smoke as a thing to be rigidly avoided, and therefore have no hesitation in accompanying their menfolk.

The observant visitor to the promenade concerts annually given in the Queen's Hall, Langham Place, will notice that but one small section of the grand circle is reserved for non-smokers, while smoking is freely allowed (with no absurd ban on the friendly pipe) in every other part of the great auditorium--floor, circle and balcony.

There are still some people who share the Duke of Wellington's delusion that smoking promotes drinking, although experience proves the contrary, and historic evidence, especially as regards drinking after dinner, shows that it was the intro-duction of the cigar, followed by that of the cigarette, which absolutely killed the old, bad after-dinner habits. The Salvation Army do not enforce total abstinence from tobacco as well as from alcoholic drinks as a condition of membership or sol-diership, but a member of the Army must be a non-smoker before he can hold any office in its rank, or be a bandsman, or a member of a "songster brigade." And in other religious organizations there are yet a few of the "unco' guid" who look askance at pipe or cigarette as if it were a device of the devil. But the numbers of these misguided folk become fewer every year.

Smoking in the dining-room after dinner is now so general that people are apt to forget that this particular development is of no great age. It is not yet, however, universal. A valued correspondent tells me that he knows a house "where tobacco is still kept out of the dining-room, and smoke indulged in elsewhere after wine. This old-fashioned habit must now be pretty rare."

The chief legitimate objection to cigarette smoking was well stated some years ago by the late Dr. Andrew Wilson. "I think cigarettes are apt to prove injurious," he said, "because a man will smoke far too much when he indulges in this form of the weed, and because I think it is generally admitted that cigarettes are apt to pro-duce evil effects out of all proportion to the amount of tobacco which is apparently consumed." Excess can equally be found among cigar and pipe-smokers. The late Chancellor Parish, in his "Dictionary of the Sussex Dialect," tells a delightful story of a Sussex rustic's holiday--"May be you knows Mass [Master, the distinctive title of a married labourer] Pilbeam? No! doaent ye? Well, he was a very sing'lar marn was Mass Pilbeam, a very sing'lar marn! He says to he's mistus one day, he says, 'tis a long time, says he, sence I've took a holiday--so cardenly, nex marnin' he laid abed till purty nigh seven o'clock, and then he brackfustes, and then he goos down to the shop and buys fower ounces of barca, and he sets hisself down on the maxon [manure heap], and there he set, and there he smoked and smoked and smoked all the whole day long, for, says he 'tis a long time sence I've had a holiday! Ah, he was a very sing'lar marn--a very sing'lar marn indeed."

Some men seem to act upon Mark Twain's principle of never smoking when asleep or at meals, and never refraining at any other time. But excess is self-condemned. There is no good reason why anyone, for social or any other reasons, should look askance at the reasonable use of tobacco. "But used in moderation, what evils, let me ask,"--I again quote Dr. Andrew Wilson's calm good sense--"are to be found in the train of the tobacco-habit! A man doesn't get delirium tremens even if he smokes more than is good for him; he doesn't become a debased mortal; there is nothing about tobacco which makes a man beat his wife or assault his mother-in-law--rather the reverse, in fact, for tobacco is a soother and a quietener of the passions, and many a man, I daresay, has been prevented from doing rash things in the way of retaliation, when he has lit his pipe and had a good think over his affairs. Whenever anybody counterblasts to-day against tobacco, I feel as did my old friend Wilkie Collins, when somebody told him that to smoke was a wrong thing. 'My dear sir,' said the great novelist, 'all your objections to tobacco only increase the relish with which I look forward to my next cigar!'"

XIII
SMOKING BY WOMEN

Ladies, when pipes are brought, affect to swoon;
They love no smoke, except the smoke of Town.
            ISAAC HAWKINS BROWNE, circa 1740.

A story is told of Sir Walter Raleigh by John Aubrey which seems to imply that at first women not only did not smoke, but that they disliked smoking by men. Aubrey says that Raleigh "standing in a stand at Sir R. Poyntz's parke at Acton, tooke a pipe of tobacco, which made the ladies quitt it till he had done." But this objection, whether general or not, soon vanished, for, as we have seen in a previous chapter, the gallant of Elizabethan and Jacobean days made a practice of smoking in his lady's presence. It seems certain, moreover, that some women, at least, smoked very soon after the introduction of tobacco; but it is not easy to find direct evidence, though there are sundry traditions and allusions which suggest that the practice was not unknown.

There is a tradition that Queen Elizabeth herself once smoked--with unpleasant results. Campbell, in his "History of Virginia," says that Raleigh having offered her Majesty "some tobacco to smoke, after two or three whiffs she was seized with a nausea, upon observing which some of the Earl of Leicester's faction whispered that Sir Walter had certainly poisoned her. But her Majesty in a short while recovering made the countess of Nottingham and all her maids smoke a whole pipe out among them." The Queen had no selfish desire to monopolize the novel sensations caused by smoking. An eighteenth-century writer, Oldys, in his "Life of Sir Walter Raleigh," declares that tobacco "soon became of such vogue in Queen Elizabeth's court, that some of the great ladies, as well as noblemen therein, would not scruple to take a pipe sometimes very sociably." But these stories rest on vague tradition, and probably have no foundation in fact.

King James I in his famous "Counter-blaste to Tobacco," hinted that the husband, by his indulgence in the habit, might "reduce thereby his delicate, wholesome, and cleane complexioned wife to that extremitie, that either shee must also corrupt her sweete breath therewith, or else resolve to live in a perpetuall stinking torment." His Majesty's style was forcible, if not elegant. There are also one or two references in the early dramatists. In Ben Jonson's "Every Man in his Humour," for instance, which was first acted in 1598, six years before King James blew his royal "Counter-blaste," Cob, the water-bearer, says that he would have any "man or woman that should but deal with a tobacco-pipe," immediately whipped. Prynne, in his attack on the stage, declared that women smoked pipes in theatres; but the truth of this statement may well be doubted. The habit was probably far from general among women, although Joshua Sylvester, a doughty opponent of the weed, was pleased to declare that "Fooles of all Sexes haunt it," i.e. tobacco.

The ballads of the period abound in rough woodcuts in which tavern scenes are often figured, wherein pewter pots and tobacco-pipes are shown lying on the table or in the hands or at the mouths of the male carousers. Men and women are figured together, but it would be very hard to find a woman in one of these rough cuts with a pipe in her hand or at her mouth. An example, in the "Shirburn Ballads" lies before me. The cut, which is very rough, heads a bacchanalian ballad characteristic of the Elizabethan period, called "A Knotte of Good Fellows," and beginning:

> Come hither, mine host, come hither!
> Come hither, mine host, come hither!
> I pray thee, mine host,
> Give us a pot and a tost,
> And let us drinke all together.

The scene is a tavern interior. Around the table are four men and a woman, while a boy approaches carrying two huge measures of ale. One man is smoking furiously, while on the table lie three other pipes--one for each man--and sundry pots and glasses. The woman is plainly a convivial soul; but there is no pipe for her, and such provision was no doubt unusual.

There is direct evidence, too, besides the story in the first paragraph of this chapter, that women disliked the prevalence of smoking. In Marston's "Antonio and Mellinda," 1602, Rosaline, when asked by her uncle when she will marry, makes the spirited reply--"Faith, kind uncle, when men abandon jealousy, forsake taking of tobacco, and cease to wear their beards so rudely long. Oh, to have a husband with a mouth continually smoking, with a bush of furs on the ridge of his chin, readie still to flop into his foaming chops, 'tis more than most intolerable;" and similar indications of dislike to smoking could be quoted from other plays.

On the other hand, it is certain that from comparatively early in the seventeenth century there were to be found here and there women who smoked.

On the title-page of Middleton's comedy, "The Roaring Girle," 1611, is a picture of the heroine, Moll Cutpurse, in man's apparel, smoking a pipe, from which a great cloud of smoke is issuing.

In the record of an early libel action brought in the court of the Archdeacon of Essex, some domestic scenes of 1621 are vividly represented. We need not trouble about the libel action, but two of the dramatis personae were a certain George Thresher, who sold beer and tobacco at his "shopp in Romford," and a good friend and customer of his named Elizabeth Savage, who, sad to say, was described as much given to "stronge drincke and tobacco." In the course of the trial, on June 8, 1621, Mistress Savage had to tell her tale, part of which is reported as follows:

"George Thresher kept a shoppe in Romford and sold tobacco there. She came divers tymes to his shoppe to buy tobacco there; and sometimes, with company of her acquaintance, did take tobacco and drincke beere in the hall of George Thresher's house, sometimes with the said George, and sometimes with his father and his brothers. And sometimes shee hath had a joint of meat and a cople of chickens dressed there; and shee, and they, and some other of her freinds, have dined there together, and paid their share for their dinner, shee being many times more willing to dine there than at an inne or taverne."

Elizabeth was evidently of a sociable turn, and though she turned her nose up at a tavern, there seems to have been little difference between these festive dinners at Mr. Thresher's "shopp," where Mistress Savage indulged her taste for ale and tobacco, and similar pleasures at an inn or tavern.

Some of the references to women smokers occur in curious connexions. When one George Glapthorne, of Whittlesey, J.P., was returned to Parliament for the Isle of Ely in 1654, his return was petitioned against, and among other charges it was said that just before the election, in a certain Martin's ale-house, he had promised to give Mrs. Martin a roll of tobacco, and had also undertaken to grant her husband a licence to brew, thus unduly influencing and corrupting the electors.

Women smokers were not confined to any one class of society. The Rev. Giles Moore, Rector of Horsted Keynes, Sussex, made a note in his journal and account book in 1665 of "Tobacco for my wyfe, 3d." As from other entries in Mr. Moore's account book we know that two ounces cost him one shilling, we may wonder what Mrs. Moore was going to do with her half-ounce. There is no other reference to tobacco for her in the journal and account book. Possibly she was not a smoker at all, but needed the tobacco for some medicinal purpose. There is ample evidence to show that in the seventeenth century extraordinary medicinal virtues continued to be attributed to the "divine weed."

In some letters of the Appleton family, printed some time ago from the originals in the Bodleian Library, there is a curious letter, undated, but of 1652 or 1653, from Susan Crane, the widow of Sir Robert Crane, who was the second wife of Isaac Appleton of Buckman Vall, Norfolk. Writing to her husband, Isaac Appleton, at his chamber in Grayes Inn, as his "Afextinat wife," the good Susan, whose spelling is marvellous, tells her "Sweet Hart"--"I have done all the tobakcre you left mee; I pray send mee sum this weeke; and some angelleco ceedd and sum cerret sed." How much tobacco Mr. Appleton had provisioned his wife with cannot be known, but it looks as if she were a regular smoker and did not care to be long without a supply. In 1631 Edmond Howes, who edited Stow's "Chronicles," and continued them "onto the end of this present yeare 1631," wrote that tobacco was "at this day commonly used by most men and many women."

Anything like general smoking by women in the seventeenth century would appear to have been confined to certain parts of the country. Celia Fiennes, who travelled about England on horseback in the reign of William and Mary, tells us that at St. Austell in Cornwall ("St. Austins," she calls it) she disliked "the custome of the country which is a universal smoking; both men, women, and children have all their pipes of tobacco in their mouths and soe sit round the fire smoking, which was not delightful to me when I went down to talk with my Landlady for information of any matter and customes amongst them." What would King James have thought of these depraved Cornish folk? Other witnesses bear testimony to the prevalence of smoking among women in the west of England. Dunton, in that Athenian Oracle *which was a kind of early forerunner of* Notes and Queries, alluded to pipe-smoking by "the good Women and Children in the West." Misson, the French traveller, who was here in 1698, after remarking that "Tabacco" is very much used in England, says that "the very Women take it in abundance, particularly in the Western Counties. But why the very *Women? What Occasion is there for that* very? We wonder that in certain Places it should be common for Women to take Tabacco; and why should we wonder at it? The Women of Devonshire and Cornwall wonder that the Women of Middlesex do not take Tabacco: And why should they wonder at it? In truth, our Wonderments are very pleasant Things!" And with that sage and satisfactory conclusion to his catechism we may leave M. Misson, though he goes on to philosophize about the effect of smoking by the English clergy upon their theology!

Another French visitor to our shores, M. Jorevin, whose rare book of travels was published at Paris in 1672, was wandering in the west of England about the year 1666, and in the course of his journey stayed at the Stag Inn at Worcester, where he found he had to make himself quite at home with the family of his hostess. He tells us that according to the custom of the country the landladies sup with strangers and passengers, and if they have daughters, these also are of the company to entertain the guests at table with pleasant conceits where they drink as much as the men. But what quite disgusted our visitor was "that when one drinks the health of any person in company, the custom of the country does not permit you to drink more than half the cup, which is filled up and presented to him or her whose health you have drunk. Moreover, the supper being finished, they set on the table half a dozen pipes, and a packet of tobacco, for smoking, which is a general custom as well among women as men, who think that without tobacco one cannot live in England, because, say they, it dissipates the evil humours of the brain."

Although, according to M. Misson, the women of Devon and Cornwall might wonder why the women of Middlesex did not take tobacco, it is certain that London and its neighbourhood did contain at least a few female smokers. Tom Brown, often dubbed "the facetious," but to whom a sterner epithet might well be applied, writing about the end of the seventeenth century, mentions a vintner's wife who, having "made her pile," as might be said nowadays, retires to a little country-house at Hampstead, where she drinks sack too plentifully, smokes tobacco in an elbow-chair, and snores away the remainder of her life. And the same writer was responsible for a satirical letter "to an Old Lady that smoak'd Tobacco," which shows that the practice was not general, for the letter begins: "Madam, Tho' the ill-natur'd world censures you for smoking." Brown advised her to continue the "innocent diversion" because, first, it was good for the toothache, "the constant persecutor of old ladies," and, secondly, it was a great help to meditation, "which is the reason, I suppose," he continues, "that recommends it to your parsons; the generality of whom can no more write a sermon without a pipe in their mouths, than a concordance in their hands."

From the evidence so far adduced it may fairly be concluded, I think, that during the seventeenth century smoking was not fashionable, or indeed anything but rare, among the women of the more well-to-do classes, while among women of humbler rank it was an occasional, and in a few districts a fairly general habit.

The same conclusion holds good for the eighteenth century. Among women of the lowest class smoking was probably common enough. In Fielding's "Amelia," a woman of the lowest character is spoken of as "smoking tobacco, drinking punch, talking obscenely and swearing and cursing"--which accomplishments are all carefully noted, because none of them would be applicable to the ordinary respectable female.

The fine lady disliked tobacco. The author of "A Pipe of Tobacco," in Dodsley's well-known "Collection," to which reference has already been made, wrote:

Ladies, when pipes are brought, affect to swoon;
They love no smoke, except the smoke of Town.

       *   *   *   *   *   *   *   *

Citronia vows it has an odious stink;
She will not smoke (ye gods!)--but she will drink;

and the same writer describes tobacco as "By ladies hated, hated by the beaux." Although the fine lady may have affected to swoon at the sight of pipes, and belles generally, like the beaux, may have disdained tobacco as vulgar, yet there were doubtless still to be found here and there respectable women who occasionally indulged in a smoke. In an early Spectator, Addison gives the rules of a "Twopenny Club, erected in this Place, for the Preservation of Friendship and good Neighbourhood," which met in a little ale-house and was frequented by artisans and mechanics. Rule II was, "Every member shall fill his pipe out of his own box"; and Rule VII was, "If any member brings his wife into the club, he shall pay for whatever she drinks or smokes."

In one of the valuable volumes issued by the Georgian Society of Dublin a year or two ago, Dr. Mahaffy, writing on the mid-eighteenth century society of the Irish capital, quotes an advertisement by a Dublin tobacconist of "mild pigtail for ladies" which suggests the alarming question--Did Irish ladies chew?

It has sometimes been supposed that the companion of Swift's Stella, Mrs. Rebecca Dingley, was addicted to smoking. In the letters which make up the famous "Journal to Stella," there are several references by Swift to the presents of tobacco which he was in the habit of sending to Mrs. Dingley. On September 21, 1710, he wrote: "I have the finest piece of Brazil tobacco for Dingley that ever was born." In the following month he again had a great piece of Brazil tobacco for the same lady, and again in November: "I have made Delaval promise to send me some Brazil tobacco from Portugal for you, Madam Dingley." In December, Swift was expressing his hope that Dingley's tobacco had not spoiled the chocolate which he had sent for Stella in the same parcel; and three months later he wrote: "No news of your box? I hope you have it, and are this minute drinking the chocolate, and that the smell of the Brazil tobacco has not affected it." The explanation of all this tobacco for Mistress Dingley is to be found in Swift's letter to Stella of October 23, 1711. "Then there's the miscellany," he writes, "an apron for Stella, a pound of chocolate, without sugar, for Stella, a fine snuff-rasp of ivory, given me by Mrs. St. John for Dingley, and a large roll of tobacco which she must hide or cut shorter out of modesty, and four pair of spectacles for the Lord knows who." The tobacco was clearly not for smoking, but for Dingley to operate upon with the snuff-rasp, and so supply herself with snuff--a luxury, which in those days, was as much enjoyed and as universally used by women as by men.

Even Quakeresses sometimes smoked. A list of the sea-stores put on board the ship in which certain friends--Samuel Fothergill, Mary Peisly, Katherine Payton and others--sailed from Philadelphia for England in June 1756, is still extant. In those days Atlantic passages were long, and might last for an indefinite period, and passengers provisioned themselves accordingly. On this occasion the passage though stormy was very quick, for it lasted only thirty-four days. The list of provisions taken is truly formidable. It includes all sorts of eatables and drinkables in astonishing quantities. The "Women's Chest," we are told, contained, among a host of other good and useful things, "Balm, sage, summer Savoury, horehound, Tobacco, and Oranges; two bottles of Brandy, two bottles of Jamaica Spirrit, A Canister of green tea, a Jar of Almond paste, Ginger bread." Samuel Fothergill's "new chest" contained tobacco among many other things; and a box of pipes was among the miscellaneous stores.

The history of smoking by women through Victorian days need not detain us long. There have always been pipe-smokers among the women of the poorer classes. Up to the middle of the last century smoking was very common among the hard-working women of Northumberland and the Scottish border. Nor has the practice by any means yet died out. In May 1913, a woman, who was charged with drunkenness at the West Ham police court, laid the blame for her condition on her pipe. She said she had smoked it for twenty years, and "it always makes me giddy!" The writer, in August 1913, saw a woman seated by the roadside in County Down, Ireland, calmly smoking a large briar pipe.

It is not so very long ago that an English traveller heard a working-man courteously ask a Scottish fish-wife, who had entered a smoking-compartment of the train, whether she objected to smoking. The good woman slowly produced a well-seasoned "cutty" pipe, and as she began to cut up a "fill" from a rank-smelling tobacco, replied: "Na, na, laddie, I've come in here for a smoke ma'sel."

The Darlington and Stockton Times in 1856 recorded the death on December 10, at Wallbury, in the North Riding of Yorkshire, in the 110th year of her age, of Jane Garbutt, widow. Mrs. Garbutt had been twice married, her husbands having been sailors during the Napoleonic wars. The old woman, said the journal, "had dwindled into a small compass, but she was free from pain, retaining all her faculties to the last, and enjoying her pipe. About a year ago the writer of this notice paid her a visit, and took her, as a 'brother-piper,' a present of tobacco, which ingredient of bliss was always acceptable from her visitors. Asking of her the question how long she had smoked, her reply was 'Vary nigh a hundred years'!" In 1845 there died at Buxton, at the age of ninety-six, a woman named Pheasy Molly, who had been for many years an inveterate smoker. Her death was caused by the accidental ignition of her clothes as she was lighting her pipe at the fire. She had burned herself more than once before in performing the same operation; but her pipe she was bound to have, and so met her end.

The old Irishwomen who were once a familiar feature of London street-life as sellers of apples and other small wares at street corners, were often hardened smokers; and so were, and doubtless still are, many of the gipsy women who tramp the country. An old Seven Dials ballad has the following choice stanza--

When first I saw Miss Bailey,
'Twas on a Saturday,
At the Corner Pin she was drinking gin,
And smoking a yard of clay.

Up to about the middle of Queen Victoria's reign female smoking in the nineteenth century in England may be said to have been pretty well confined to women of the classes and type already mentioned. Respectable folk in the middle and upper classes would have been horrified at the idea of a pipe or a cigar between feminine lips; and cigarettes had been used by men for a long time before it began to be whispered that here and there a lady--who was usually considered dreadfully "fast" for her pains--was accustomed to venture upon a cigarette.

In "Puck," 1870, Ouida represented one of her beautiful young men, Vy Bruce, as "murmuring idlest nonsense to Lilian Lee, as he lighted one of his cigarettes for her use"--but Lilian Lee was a cocotte.

An amusing incident is related in Forster's "Life of Dickens," which shows how entirely unknown was smoking among women of the middle and upper classes in England some ten years after Queen Victoria came to the throne. Dickens was at Lausanne and Geneva in the autumn of 1846. At his hotel in Geneva he met a remarkable mother and daughter, both English, who admired him greatly, and whom he had previously known at Genoa. The younger lady's conversation would have shocked the prim maids and matrons of that day. She asked Dickens if he had ever "read such infernal trash" as Mrs. Gore's; and exclaimed "Oh God! what a sermon we had here, last Sunday." Dickens and his two daughters--"who were decidedly in the way, as we agreed afterwards"--dined by invitation with the mother and daughter. The daughter asked him if he smoked. "Yes," said Dickens, "I generally take a cigar after dinner when I'm alone." Thereupon said the young lady, "I'll give you a good 'un when we go upstairs." But the sequel must be told in the novelist's own inimitable style. "Well, sir," he wrote, "in due course we went upstairs, and there we were joined by an American lady residing in the same hotel ... also a daughter ... American lady married at sixteen; American daughter sixteen now, often mistaken for sisters, &c. &c. &c. When that was over, the younger of our entertainers brought out a cigar-box, and gave me a cigar, made of negrohead she said, which would quell an elephant in six whiffs. The box was full of cigarettes--good large ones, made of pretty strong tobacco; I always smoke them here, and used to smoke them at Genoa, and I knew them well. When I lighted my cigar, daughter lighted hers, at mine; leaned against the mantelpiece, in conversation with me; put out her stomach, folded her arms, and with her pretty face cocked up sideways and her cigarette smoking away like a Manchester cotton mill, laughed, and talked, and smoked, in the most gentlemanly manner I ever beheld. Mother immediately lighted her cigar; American lady immediately lighted hers; and in five minutes the room was a cloud of smoke, with us four in the centre pulling away bravely, while American lady related stories of her 'Hookah' upstairs, and described different kinds of pipes. But even this was not all. For presently two Frenchmen came in, with whom, and the American lady, daughter sat down to whist. The Frenchmen smoked of course (they were really modest gentlemen and seemed dismayed), and daughter played for the next hour or two with a cigar continually in her mouth--never out of it. She certainly smoked six or eight. Mother gave in soon--I think she only did it out of vanity. American lady had been smoking all the morning. I took no more; and daughter and the Frenchmen had it all to themselves. Conceive this in a great hotel, with not only their own servants, but half a dozen waiters coming constantly in and out! I showed no atom of surprise, but I never was so surprised, so ridiculously taken aback, in my life; for in all my experience of 'ladies' of one kind and another, I never saw a woman--not a basket woman or a gipsy--smoke before!" This last remark is highly significant. Forster says that Dickens "lived to have larger and wider experience, but there was enough to startle as well as amuse him in the scene described." The words "cigar" and "cigarette" are used indifferently by the novelist, but it seems clear from the description and from the number smoked by the lady in an hour or two, that it was a cigarette and not a cigar, properly so called, which was never out of her mouth.

The ladies who so surprised Dickens were English and American, but at the period in question--the early 'forties of the last century--one of the freaks of fashion at Paris was the giving of luncheon parties for ladies only, at which cigars were handed round.

The first hints of feminine smoking in England may be traced, like so many other changes in fashion, in the pages of Punch. In 1851, steady-going folk were alarmed and shocked at a sudden and short-lived outburst of "bloomerism," imported from the United States. Of course it was at once suggested that women who would go so far as to imitate masculine attire and to emancipate themselves from the usual conventions of feminine dress, would naturally seek to imitate men in other ways also. Leech had a picture of "A Quiet Smoke" in Punch, which depicted five ladies in short wide skirts and "bloomers" in a tobacconist's shop, two smoking cigars and one a pipe, while "one of the inferior animals" behind the counter was selling tobacco. But this was satire and hardly had much relation to fact.

It was not until the 'sixties of the last century that cigarette-smoking by women began to creep in. Mortimer Collins, writing in 1869, in a curious outburst against the use of tobacco by young men, said, "When one hears of sly cigarettes between feminine lips at croquet parties, there is no more to be said." Since that date cigarette-smoking has become increasingly popular among women, and the term "sly" has long ceased to be applicable. "Punch's Pocket-Book" for 1878 had an amusing skit on a ladies' reading-party, to which Mr. Punch acted as "coach." After breakfast the reading ladies lounged on the lawn with cigarettes.

What Queen Victoria, who hated tobacco and banished it from her presence and from her abodes as far as she could, would have thought and said of the extent to which cigarette-smoking is indulged in now by women, is a question quite unanswerable. Yet Queen Victoria once received a present of pipes and tobacco. By the hands of Sir Richard Burton the Queen had sent a damask tent, a silver pipe, and two silver trays to the King of Dahomey. That potentate told Sir Richard that the tent was very handsome, but too small; that the silver pipe did not smoke so well as his old red clay with a wooden stem; and that though he liked the trays very much, he thought them hardly large enough to serve as shields. He hoped that the next gifts would include a carriage and pair, and a white woman, both of which he would appreciate very much. However, he sent gifts in return to her Britannic Majesty, and among them were a West African state umbrella, a selection of highly coloured clothing materials, and some native pipes and tobacco for the Queen to smoke.

Many royal ladies of Europe, contemporaries of Queen Victoria and her son, have had the reputation of being confirmed smokers. Among them may be named Carmen Sylva, the poetess--Queen of Roumania, the Dowager Tsaritsa of Russia, the late Empress of Austria, King Alfonso's mother, formerly Queen-Regent of Spain, the Dowager Queen Margherita of Italy and ex-Queen Amelie of Portugal. It is, of course, well known that Austrian and Russian ladies generally are fond of cigarette-smoking. On Russian railways it is not unusual to find a compartment labelled "For ladies who do not smoke."

The newspapers reported not long ago from the other side of the Atlantic that the "smart" women of Chicago had substituted cigars for cigarettes. According to an interview with a Chicago hotel proprietor, the fair smokers "select their cigars as men do, either black and strong, or light, according to taste." How in the world else could they select them? It is not likely, however, that cigar-smoking will become popular among women. For one thing, it leaves too strong and too clinging an odour on the clothes.

One of the latest announcements, however, in the fashion pages of the news-papers is the advent of "Smoking Jackets" for ladies! We are informed in the usual style of such pages, that "the well-dressed woman has begun to consider the little smoking-jacket indispensable." This jacket, we are told "is a very different matter to the braided velvet coats which were donned by our masculine forbears in the days of long drooping cavalry moustaches, tightly buttoned frock-coats, and flex-ible canes. The feminine smoking-jacket of to-day is worn with entrancing little evening or semi-evening frocks, and represents a compromise between a cloak and a coat, being exquisitely draped and fashioned of the softest and most attractive of the season's beautiful fabrics."

There are still many good people nowadays who are shocked at the idea of women smoking; and to them may be commended the common-sense words of Bishop Boyd-Carpenter, formerly of Ripon, who arrived in New York early in 1913 to deliver a series of lectures at Harvard University. The American newspapers reported him as saying, with reference to this subject: "Many women in England who are well thought of, smoke. I do not attempt to enter into the ethical part of this matter, but this much I say: if men find it such a pleasure to smoke, why shouldn't women? There are many colours in the rainbow; so there are many tastes in people. What may be a pleasure to men may be given to women. When we find women smoking, as they do in some branches of society to-day, the mere pleasure of that habit must be accepted as belonging to both sexes."

XIV
SMOKING IN CHURCH

For thy sake, TOBACCO, I
Would do anything but die.
CHARLES LAMB, A Farewell to Tobacco.

The use of tobacco in churches forms a curious if short chapter in the social history of smoking. The earliest reference to such a practice occurs in 1590, when Pope Innocent XII excommunicated all such persons as were found taking snuff or using tobacco in any form in the church of St. Peter, at Rome; and again in 1624, Pope Urban VIII issued a bull against the use of tobacco in churches.

In England it would seem as if some of the early smokers, in the fulness of their enthusiasm for the new indulgence, went so far as to smoke in church. When King James I was about to visit Cambridge, the Vice-Chancellor of the University put forth sundry regulations in connexion with the royal visit, in which may be found the following passage: "That noe Graduate, Scholler, or Student of this Universitie presume to resort to any Inn, Taverne, Alehowse, or Tobacco-Shop at any tyme dureing the aboade of his Majestie here; nor doe presume to take tobacco in St. Marie's Church, or in Trinity Colledge Hall, uppon payne of finall expellinge the Universitie."

Evidently the intention was to make things pleasant for the royal foe of tobacco during his visit. It would appear to be a fair inference from the wording of this prohibition that when the King was not at Cambridge, graduates and scholars and students could resume their liberty to resort to inns, taverns, ale-houses and tobacco-shops, and presumably to take tobacco in St. Mary's Church, without question.

The prohibition, in the regulation quoted, of smoking in St. Mary's Church, referred, it may be noted, to the Act which was held therein. Candidates for degrees, or graduates to display their proficiency, publicly maintained theses; and this performance was termed keeping or holding an Act.

It is, of course, conceivable that the prohibition, so far as the church and Trinity College Hall were concerned, was against the taking of snuff rather than against smoking; but the phrase "to take tobacco" was at that time quite commonly applied to smoking, and, considering the extraordinary and immoderate use of tobacco soon after its introduction, it is not in the least incredible that pipes were lighted, at least occasionally, even in sacred buildings.

Sometimes tobacco was used in church for disinfecting or deodorizing purposes. The churchwardens' accounts of St. Peter's, Barnstaple, for 1741 contain the entry: "Pd. for Tobacco and Frankincense burnt in the Church 2s. 6d." Sprigs of juniper, pitch, and "sweete wood," in combination with incense, were often used for the same purpose.

Smoking, it may safely be asserted, was never practised commonly in English churches. Even in our own day people have been observed smoking--not during service time, but in passing through the building--in church in some of the South American States, and nearer home in Holland; but in England such desecration has been occasional only, and quite exceptional.

One need not be much surprised at any instance of lack of reverence in English churches during the eighteenth century, and a few instances can be given of church smoking in that era.

Blackburn, Archbishop of York, was a great smoker. On one occasion he was at St. Mary's Church, Nottingham, for a confirmation. The story of what happened was told long afterwards in a letter written in December 1773 by John Disney, rector of Swinderby, Lincolnshire, the grandson of the Mr. Disney who at the time of the Archbishop's visit to St. Mary's was incumbent of that church. This letter was addressed to James Granger, and was published in Granger's correspondence. "The anecdote which you mention," wrote the Mr. Disney of Swinderby, "is, I believe, unquestionably true. The affair happened in St. Mary's Church at Nottingham, when Archbishop Blackbourn (of York) was there on a visitation. The Archbishop had ordered some of the apparitors, or other attendants, to bring him pipes and tobacco, and some liquor into the vestry for his refreshment after the fatigue of confirmation. And this coming to Mr. Disney's ears, he forbad them being brought thither, and with a becoming spirit remonstrated with the Archbishop upon the impropriety of his conduct, at the same time telling his Grace that his vestry should not be converted into a smoking-room."

Another eighteenth-century clerical worthy, the famous Dr. Parr, an inveterate smoker, was accustomed to do what Mr. Disney prevented Archbishop Blackburn from doing--he smoked in his vestry at Hatton. This he did before the sermon, while the congregation were singing a hymn, and apparently both parties were pleased, for Parr would say: "My people like long hymns; but I prefer a long clay."

Robert Hall, the famous Baptist preacher, having once upon a time strongly denounced smoking as an "odious custom," learned to smoke himself as a result of his acquaintance with Dr. Parr. Parr was such a continual smoker that anyone who came into his company, if he had never smoked before, had to learn the use of a pipe as a means of self-defence. Hall, who became a heavy smoker, is said to have smoked in his vestry at intervals in the service. He probably found some relief in tobacco from the severe internal pains with which for many years he was afflicted.

Mr. Ditchfield, in his entertaining book on "The Parish Clerk," tells a story of a Lincolnshire curate who was a great smoker, and who, like Parr, was accustomed to retire to the vestry before the sermon and there smoke a pipe while the congregation sang a psalm. "One Sunday," says Mr. Ditchfield, "he had an extra pipe, and Joshua (the clerk) told him that the people were getting impatient.

"'Let them sing another psalm,' said the curate.

"'They have, sir,' replied the clerk.

"'Then let them sing the hundred and nineteenth,' replied the curate.

"At last he finished his pipe, and began to put on the black gown, but its folds were troublesome and he could not get it on.

"'I think the devil's in the gown,' muttered the curate.

"'I think he be,' dryly replied old Joshua."

The same writer, in his companion volume on "The Old Time Parson," mentions that the Vicar of Codrington in 1692 found that it was actually customary for people to play cards on the Communion Table, and that "when they chose the churchwardens they used to sit in the Sanctuary smoking and drinking, the clerk gravely saying, with a pipe in his mouth, that such had been their custom for the last sixty years."

Although probably the conduct of the Codrington parishioners was unusual, it is certain that in the seventeenth century smoking at meetings held, not in the church itself, but in the vestry, was common. The churchwardens' accounts of St. Mary, Leicester, 1665-6, record the expenditure--"In beer and tobacco from first to last 7s. 10d." In those of St. Alphege, London Wall, for 1671, there are the entries--"For Pipes and Tobaccoe in the Vestry 2s.," and "For a grosse of pipes at severall times 2s." In the next century, however, the practice was modified. The St. Alphege accounts for 1739 have the entry--"Ordered that there be no Smoking nor Drinking for the future in the Vestry Room during the time business is doing on pain of forfeiting one shilling, Assention Day excepted." From this it would seem fair to infer (1) that there was no objection to the lighting of pipes in the vestry after the business of the meeting had been transacted; and (2) that on Ascension Day for some inscrutable reason there was no prohibition at all of "Smoking and Drinking."

Readers of Sir Walter Scott will remember in "The Heart of Midlothian" one curious instance of eighteenth-century smoking in church--in a Scottish Presbyterian church, too. Jeanie Deans's beloved Reuben Butler was about to be ordained to the charge of the parish of Knocktarlitie, Dumbartonshire; the congregation were duly seated, after prayers, douce David Deans occupying a seat among the elders, and the officiating minister had read his text preparatory to the delivery of his hour and a quarter sermon. The redoubtable Duncan of Knockdunder was making his preparations also for the sermon. "After rummaging the leathern purse which hung in front of his petticoat, he produced a short tobacco-pipe made of iron, and observed almost aloud, 'I hae forgotten my spleuchan--Lachlan, gang doon to the Clachan, and bring me up a pennyworth of twist.' Six arms, the nearest within reach, presented, with an obedient start, as many tobacco-pouches to the man of office. He made choice of one with a nod of acknowledgment, filled his pipe, lighted it with the assistance of his pistol-flint, and smoked with infinite composure during the whole time of the sermon. When the discourse was finished, he knocked the ashes out of his pipe, replaced it in his sporran, returned the tobacco-pouch or spleuchan to its owner, and joined in the prayers with decency and attention." David Deans, however, did not at all approve this irreverence. "It didna become a wild Indian," he said, "much less a Christian and a gentleman, to sit in the kirk puffing tobacco-reek, as if he were in a change-house." The date of the incident was 1737; but whether Sir Walter had any authority in fact for this characteristic performance of Knockdunder, or not, it is certain that any such occurrence in a Scottish kirk must have been extremely rare.

Knockdunder's pipe, according to Scott, was made of iron. This was an infrequent material for tobacco-pipes, but there are a few examples in museums. In the Belfast Museum there is a cast iron tobacco-pipe about eighteen inches long. With it are shown another, very short, also of cast iron, the bowl of a brass pipe, and a pipe, about six inches in length, made of sheet iron.

Another eighteenth-century instance of smoking in church, taken from historical fact and not from fiction, is associated with the church of Hayes, in Middlesex. The parish registers of that village bear witness to repeated disputes between the parson and bell-ringers and the parishioners generally in 1748-1754. In 1752 it was noted that a sermon had been preached after a funeral "to a noisy congregation." On another occasion, says the register, "the ringers and other inhabitants disturbed the service from the beginning of prayers to the end of the sermon, by ringing the bells, and going into the gallery to spit below"; while at yet another time "a fellow came into church with a pot of beer and a pipe," and remained "smoking in his own pew until the end of the sermon." Going to church at Hayes in those days must have been quite an exciting experience. No one knew what might happen next.

In remote English and Welsh parishes men seem occasionally to have smoked in churches without any intention of being irreverent, and without any consciousness that they were doing anything unusual. Canon Atkinson, in his delightful book "Forty Years in a Moorland Parish," tells how, when he first went to Danby in Cleveland--then very remote from the great world--and had to take his first funeral, he found inside the church the parish clerk, who was also parish schoolmaster by the way, sitting in the sunny embrasure of the west window with his hat on and comfortably smoking his pipe. A correspondent of the Times in 1895 mentioned that his mother had told him how she remembered seeing smoking in a Welsh church about 1850--"The Communion table stood in the aisle, and the farmers were in the habit of putting their hats upon it, and when the sermon began they lit their pipes and smoked, but without any idea of irreverence." In an Essex church about 1861, a visitor had pointed out to him various nooks in the gallery where short pipes were stowed away, which he was informed the old men smoked during service; and several of the pews in the body of the church contained triangular wooden spittoons filled with sawdust.

A clergyman has put it on record that when he went in 1873 as curate-in-charge to an out-of-the-way Norfolk village, at his first early celebration he arrived in church about 7.45 A.M., and, he says, "to my amazement saw five old men sitting round the stove in the nave with their hats on, smoking their pipes. I expostulated with them quite quietly, but they left the church before service and never came again. I discovered afterwards that they had been regular communicants, and that my predecessor always distributed the offertory to the poor present immediately after the service. When these men, in the course of my remonstrance found that I was not going to continue the custom, they no longer cared to be communicants."

Nowadays, if smoking takes place in church at all, it can only be done with intentional irreverence; and it is painful to think that even at the present day there are people in whom a feeling of reverence and decency is so far lacking as to lead them to desecrate places of worship. The Vicar of Lancaster, at his Easter vestry meeting in 1913, complained of bank-holiday visitors to the parish church who ate their lunch, smoked, and wore their hats while looking round the building. It is absurd to suppose that these people were unconscious of the impropriety of their conduct.

XV
TOBACCONISTS' SIGNS

S hop-signs were one of the most conspicuous features of the streets of old
London. In days when the numbering of houses was unknown, the use of
signs was indispensable for identification; and greatly must they have contributed to the quaint and picturesque appearance of the streets. Some pro-
jected far over the narrow roadway--competition to attract attention and custom is
no modern novelty--some were fastened to posts or pillars in front of the houses.
By the time of Charles II the overhanging signs had become a nuisance and a danger, and in the seventh year of that King's reign an Act was passed providing that
no sign should hang across the street, but that all should be fixed to the balconies
or fronts or sides of houses. This Act was not strictly obeyed; and large numbers of
signs were hung over the doors, while many others were affixed to the fronts of the
houses. Eventually, in the second half of the eighteenth century, signs gradually
disappeared and the streets were numbered. There were occasional survivals which
are to be found to this day, such as the barber's pole, accompanied sometimes by
the brass basin of the barber-surgeon, the glorified canister of a grocer or the golden
leg of a hosier; and inn signs have never failed us; but by the close of the eighteenth
century most of the old trade signs which flaunted themselves in the streets had
disappeared.

The sellers of tobacco naturally hung out their signs like other tradesfolk. Signs
in their early days were, no doubt, chosen to intimate the trades of those who used

them, and in the easy-going old-fashioned days when it was considered the right and natural thing for a son to be brought up to his father's trade and to succeed him therein, they long remained appropriate and intelligible. Later, as we shall see, they became meaningless in many cases. But in the days when tobacco-smoking first came into vogue, the signs chosen naturally had some reference to the trade they indicated, and one of the earliest used was the sign of the "Black Boy," in allusion to the association of the negro with tobacco cultivation. The "Black Boy" existed as a shop-sign before tobacco's triumph, for Henry Machyn in his "Diary," so early as December 30, 1562, mentions a goldsmith "dwellying at the sene of the Blake Boy, in the Cheep"; but the early sellers of tobacco soon fastened on this appropriate sign. The earliest reference to such use may be found in Ben Jonson's "Bartholomew Fair," 1614, where, in the first scene, Humphrey Waspe says: "I thought he would have run mad o' the Black Boy in Bucklersbury, that takes the scurvy, roguy tobacco there." Later, the "Black Boy," like other once significant signs, became meaningless and was used in connexion with various trades. Early in the eighteenth century a bookseller at the sign of the "Black Boy" on London Bridge was advertising Defoe's "Robinson Crusoe"; another bookseller traded at the "Black Boy" in Paternoster Row in 1712. Linendrapers, hatters, pawnbrokers and other tradesmen all used the same sign at various dates in the eighteenth century. But side by side with this indiscriminate and unnecessary use of the sign there existed a continuous association of the "Black Boy" with the tobacco trade. A tobacconist named Milward lived at the "Black Boy" in Redcross Street, Barbican, in 1742; and many old tobacco papers show a black boy, or sometimes two, smoking. Mr. Holden MacMichael, in his papers on "The London Signs" says: "Mrs. Skinner, of the old-established tobacconist's opposite the Law Courts in the Strand, possessed, about the year 1890, two signs of the 'Black Boy,' appertaining, no doubt, to the old house of Messrs. Skinner's on Holborn Hill, of the front of which there is an illustration in the Archer Collection in the Print Department of the British Museum, where the black boy and tobacco-rolls are depicted outside the premises." The "Black Boy," indeed, continued in use by tobacconists until the nineteenth century was well advanced. A tobacconist had a shop "uppon Wapping Wall" in 1667 at the sign of the "Black Boy and Pelican."

Other significant early tobacconists' signs were "Sir Walter Raleigh," "The Virginian" and "The Tobacco Roll." "Sir Walter," as the reputed introducer of tobacco, was naturally chosen as a sign, and his portrait adorns several shop-bills in the Banks Collection. The American Indians, represented under the figure of "The Virginian," and the negroes were hopelessly confused by the early tobacconists, with results which were sometimes surprising from an ethnological point of view. As the first tobacco imported into this country came from Virginia, a supposed "Virginian" was naturally adopted as a tobacco-seller's sign at an early date. An "Indian" or a "Negro" or a figure which was a combination of both, was commonly represented wearing a kilt or a girdle of tobacco leaves, a feathered head-dress, and smoking a pipe. A tobacco-paper, dating from about the time of Queen Anne, bears rudely engraved the figure of a negro smoking, and holding a roll of tobacco in his hand. Above his head is a crown; behind are two ships in full sail, with the sun just appearing from the right-hand corner above. The foreground shows four little black boys planting and packing tobacco, and below them is the name of the ingenious tradesman--"John Winkley, Tobacconist, near ye Bridge, in the Burrough, Southwark." Sixty years or so ago a wooden figure, representing a negro with a gilt loincloth and band with feathered head, and sometimes with a tobacco roll, was still a frequent ornament of tobacconists' shops.

The "Tobacco Roll," either alone or in various combinations, was one of the commonest of early tobacconists' signs, and was in constant use for a couple of centuries. It may still be occasionally seen at the present time in the form of the "twist" with alternate brown or black and yellow coils, which up to quite a recent date was a tolerably frequent adornment of tobacconists' shops, but is now rare. This roll represented what was called spun or twist tobacco. Dekker, in James I's time, speaks of roll tobacco. The youngster who mimics the stage-gallants in Jonson's "Cynthia's Revels" as described in Chapter II (ante; page 31), says that he has "three sorts of tobacco in his pocket," which probably means that it was customary to mix for smoking purposes tobacco of the three usual kinds--roll (or pudding), leaf and cane. One would have thought that a representation of the tobacco plant itself would have been a more natural and comprehensive sign than one particular preparation of the herb, yet representations of the plant were rare, while those of the compressed tobacco known as pudding or roll in the form of a "Tobacco Roll," as described above, were very frequently used as signs.

From the examples given in Burn's "Descriptive Catalogue of London Tokens" of the seventeenth century, it is clear that the "Tobacco Roll" was a warm favourite. "Three Tobacco Rolls" was also used as a sign. In 1732 there was a "Tobacco Roll" in Finch Lane, on the north side of Cornhill, "over against the Swan and Rummer Tavern." In 1766, Mrs. Flight, tobacconist, carried on her business at the "Tobacco Roll. Next door but one to St. Christopher's Church, Threadneedle Street."

The shop-bill of Richard Lee, who sold tobacco about 1730 "at Ye Golden Tobacco Roll in Panton Street near Leicester Fields," is an elaborate production. Hogarth in the earlier period of his career as an engraver engraved many shop-bills, and this particular bill is usually attributed to him, though the attribution has been disputed. There is a copy of the bill in the British Museum, and in the catalogue of the prints and drawings in the National Collection Mr. Stephens thus describes it: "It is an oblong enclosing an oval, the spandrels being occupied by leaves of the tobacco plant tied in bundles; the above title (Richard Lee at Ye Golden Tobacco Roll in Panton Street near Leicester Fields) is on a frame which encloses the oval. Within the latter the design represents the interior of a room, with ten gentlemen gathered near a round table on which is a bowl of punch; several of the gentlemen are smoking tobacco in long pipes; one of them stands up on our right and vomits; another, who is intoxicated, lies on the floor by the side of a chair; a fire of wood burns in the grate; on the wall hangs two pictures ... three men's hats hang on pegs on the wall." Altogether this is an interesting and suggestive design, but hardly in the taste likely to commend itself to present day tradesmen.

A roll of tobacco, it may be noted, was a common form of payment to the Fleet parsons for their scoundrelly services. Pennant, writing in 1791, describes how these men hung out their frequent signs of a male and female hand conjoined, with the legend written below: "Marriages performed within." Before his shop walked the parson--"a squalid, profligate figure, clad in a tattered plaid nightgown, with a fiery face, and ready to couple you for a dram of gin, or roll of tobacco."

Combinations of the roll in tobacconists' signs occur occasionally. In 1660 there was a "Tobacco Roll and Sugar Loaf" at Gray's Inn Gate, Holborn. In 1659 James Barnes issued a farthing token from the "Sugar Loaf and Three Tobacco Rolls" in the Poultry, London. The "Sugar Loaf" was the principal grocer's sign, and so when it is found in combination with the tobacco roll at this time it may reasonably be assumed that the proprietor of the business was a grocer who was also a tobacconist.

Before the end of the seventeenth century, however, the signs were ceasing to have any necessary association with the trade carried on under them, and tobacconists are found with shop-signs which had no reference in any way to tobacco. For instance, to take a few examples from the late Mr. Hilton Price's lists of "Signs of Old London" from Cheapside and adjacent streets, in 1695 John Arundell, tobacconist, was at the "White Horse," Wood Street; in the same year J. Mumford, tobacconist, was at the "Faulcon," Laurence Lane; in 1699 Mr. Brutton, tobacconist, was to be found at the "Three Crowns," under the Royal Exchange; in 1702 Richard Bronas, tobacconist, was at the "Horse Shoe," Bread Street; and in 1766 Mr. Hoppie, of the "Oil Jar: Old Change, Watling Street End," advertised that he "sold a newly invented phosphorus powder for lighting pipes quickly in about half a minute. Ask for a Bottle of Thunder Powder."

Again, in Fleet Street, Mr. Townsend, tobacconist, traded in 1672 at the "Three Golden Balls," near St. Dunstan's Church; while at the end of Fetter Lane, a few years later, John Newland, tobacconist, was to be found at the "King's Head."

Addison, in the twenty-eighth Spectator, April 2, 1711, took note of the severance which had taken place between sign and trade, and of the absurdity that the sign no longer had any significance. After satirizing first, the monstrous conjunctions in signs of "Dog and Gridiron," "Cat and Fiddle" and so forth; and next the absurd custom by which young tradesmen, at their first starting in business, added their own signs to those of the masters under whom they had served their apprenticeship; the essayist goes on to say: "In the third place I would enjoin every shop to make use of a sign which bears some affinity to the wares in which it deals. What can be more inconsistent than to see ... a tailor at the Lion? A cook should not live at the Boot, nor a Shoe-maker at the Roasted Pig; and yet for want of this regulation, I have seen a Goat set up before the door of a perfumer, and the French King's Head at a sword-cutler's."

Notwithstanding the few examples given above, tobacconists, more than most tradesmen, seem to have continued to use signs that had at least some relevance to their trade. Abel Drugger was a "tobacco-man," i.e. a tobacco-seller in Ben Jonson's play of "The Alchemist," 1610, so that it is not very surprising to find the name used occasionally as a tobacconist's sign. Towards the end of the eighteenth century one Peter Cockburn traded as a tobacconist at the sign of the "Abel Drugger" in

Fenchurch Street, and informed the public on the advertising papers in which he wrapped up his tobacco for customers that he had formerly been shopman at the Sir Roger de Coverley--a notice which has preserved the name of another tobacconist's sign borrowed from literature. Seventeenth--century London signs were the "Three Tobacco Pipes," "Two Tobacco Pipes" crossed, and "Five Tobacco Pipes." At Edinburgh in the eighteenth century there were tobacconists who used two pipes crossed, a roll of tobacco and two leaves over two crossed pipes, and a roll of tobacco and three leaves.

The older tobacconists were wont to assert, says Larwood, that the man in the moon could enjoy his pipe, hence "the 'Man in the Moon' is represented on some of the tobacconists' papers in the Banks Collection puffing like a steam engine, and underneath the words, 'Who'll smoake with ye Man in ye Moone?'" The Dutch, as every one knows, are great smokers, so a Dutchman has been a common figure on tobacconists' signs. In the eighteenth century a common device was three figures representing a Dutchman, a Scotchman and a sailor, explained by the accompanying rhyme:

> We three are engaged in one cause,
> I snuffs, I smokes, and I chaws!

Larwood says that a tobacconist in the Kingsland Road had the three men on his sign, but with a different legend:

> This Indian weed is good indeed,
> Puff on, keep up the joke
> 'Tis the best, 'twill stand the test,
> Either to chew or smoke.

The bill bearing this sign is in Banks's Collection, 1750. Another in the same collection, with a similar meaning but of more elaborate design, shows the three men, the central figure having his hands in his pockets and in his mouth a pipe from which smoke is rolling. The man on the left advances towards this central figure holding out a pipe, above which is the legend "Voule vous de Rape." Above the middle man is "No dis been better." The third man, on the right, holds out, also towards the central figure, a tobacco-box, above which is the legend "Will you have a quid."

A frequent sign-device among dealers in snuff was the Crown and Rasp. The oldest method of taking snuff, says Larwood, in the "History of Signboards," was "to scrape it with a rasp from the dry root of the tobacco plant; the powder was then placed on the back of the hand and so snuffed up; hence the name of rape (rasped) for a kind of snuff, and the common tobacconist's sign of La Carotte d'or (the golden root) in France." Rape *became in English "rappee," familiar in snuff-taking days as the name for a coarse kind of snuff made from the darker and ranker tobacco leaves. The list of prices and names given by Wimble, a snuff-seller, about 1740, and printed in Fairholt's "History of Tobacco," contains eighteen different kinds of rappee--English, best English, fine English, high-flavoured coarse, low, scented, composite, &c. The rasps for obtaining this* rape, continues Larwood, "were carried in the waistcoat pocket, and soon became articles of luxury, being carved in ivory and variously enriched. Some of them, in ivory and inlaid wood, may be seen at the Hotel Cluny in Paris, and an engraving of such an object occurs in 'Archaeologia,' vol. xiii. One of the first snuff-boxes was the so-called rape *or* grivoise box, at the back of which was a little space for a piece of the root, whilst a small iron rasp was contained in the middle. When a pinch was wanted, the root was drawn a few times over the iron rasp, and so the snuff was produced and could be offered to a friend with much more grace than under the above-mentioned process with the pocket-grater."

The tobacconists' sign that for very many years was in most general use was the figure of a highlander, which may still perhaps be found in one or two places, but which was not at all an unusual sight in the streets of London and other towns some forty or fifty years ago. Most men of middle age can remember when the snuff-taking highlander was the usual ornament to the entrance of a tobacconist's shop; but all have disappeared from London streets save two--I say two on the authority of Mr. E.V. Lucas, who gives it (in his "Wanderer in London") as the number of the survivors; but only one is known to me. This is the famous old wooden highlander which stood for more than a hundred years on guard at a tobacconist's shop in Tottenham Court Road. About the end of 1906 it was announced that the shop was to be demolished, and that the time-worn figure was for sale. The announcement created no small stir, and it was said that the offers for the highlander ran up to a surprising figure. He was bought ultimately by a neighbouring furnishing firm, and now stands on duty not far from his ancient post, though no passer-by can help feeling the incongruity between the time-honoured emblem of the snuff-taker and his present surroundings of linoleum "and sich."

Where Mr. Lucas's second survivor may be is unknown to me. Not so many years ago a wooden highlander, as a tobacconist's sign, was a conspicuous figure in Knightsbridge, and there was another in the Westminster Bridge Road; but tempus edax rerum has consumed them with all their brethren. In a few provincial towns a wooden highlander may still be found at the door of tobacco shops, but they are probably destined to early disappearance. In 1907 one still stood guard--a tall figure in full costume--outside a tobacconist's shop in Cheltenham, and may still be there. There is a highlander of oak in the costume of the Black Watch still standing, I believe, in the doorway of a tobacco shop at St. Heliers, Jersey. It is traditionally said to have been originally the figure-head of a war vessel which was wrecked on the Alderney coast. Another survivor may be seen at the door of a shop belonging to Messrs. Churchman, tobacco manufacturers, in Westgate Street, Ipswich. A correspondent of "Notes and Queries" describes it as a very fine specimen in excellent condition, and adds: "Mr. W. Churchman informs me that it belonged to his grandfather, who established the business in Ipswich in 1790, and he believed it was quite 'a hundred' year old at that time."

One of the earliest known examples of these highlanders as tobacconists' signs is that which was placed at the door of a shop in Coventry Street which was opened in 1720 under the sign of "The Highlander, Thistle and Crown." This is said to have been a favourite place of resort of the Jacobites. In his "Nicotine and its Rariora," Mr. A.M. Broadley gives the card, dated 1765, of "William Kebb, at ye Highlander ye corner of Pall Mall, facing St. James's, Haymarket," and says that the highlander was a favourite tobacconist's sign for 200 years. I have been unable, however, to find evidence of such a prolonged period of favour. I know of no certain seventeenth-century reference to the highlander as a tobacconist's sign.

The figure was usually made with a snuff mull in his hand--the highlander being always credited with a great love and a great capacity for snuff-taking. But one curious example was furnished, not only with a mull but with a bat-like implement of unknown use. Mr. Arthur Denman, F.S.A., writing in Notes and Queries, April 17, 1909, said: "I have a very neat little, genuine specimen of the old tobacconist's sign of a 42nd Highlander with his 'mull.' It is 3 ft. 6 in. high, and it differs from those usually met with in that under the left arm is an implement almost exactly like a cricket-bat. This bat has a gilt knob to the handle, and on the shoulder of it are three chevrons in gold, without doubt a sergeant's stripes. On the exposed side of the bat is what would appear to represent a loose strip of wood. This strip is nearly one-third of the width of the instrument, and extends up the middle about two-fifths of the length of the body of it. I can only guess that the bat was, at some time, primarily, an emblem of a sergeant's office, and, secondarily, used for the infliction of chastisement on clumsy or disorderly recruits; and perhaps it was equivalent to the Pruegel of German armies, with which sergeants drove lagging warriors into the fray. But is there any record of such an accoutrement as being that of a sergeant in the British army? and what was the purpose of the loose strip, unless it was to cause the blow administered to resound as much as to hurt, as does the wand of Harlequin in a booth."

These questions received no answers from the learned correspondents of the most useful and omniscient of weekly papers. Personally, I much doubt Mr. Denman's suggested explanations of his highlander's curious implement. There is no evidence that a sergeant in the British army ever carried a cricket-bat-like implement either as a sign of office or to be used for disciplinary or punitive purposes like the canes of the German sergeants of long ago. It would seem to be more likely that this particular figure was of unusual, perhaps unique, make, and had some special local or individual significance, wherever or for whom it was first made and used, which has now been forgotten.

After the suppression of the Jacobite uprising of 1745, the English Government made war on Scottish nationality, and among other measures the wearing of the highland dress was forbidden by Parliament. On this occasion the following paragraph appeared in the newspapers of the time: "We hear that the dapper wooden Highlanders, who guard so heroically the doors of snuff-shops, intend to petition the Legislature, in order that they may be excused from complying with the Act of Parliament with regard to their change of dress: alledging that they have ever been faithful subjects to his Majesty, having constantly supplied his Guards with a pinch out of their Mulls when they marched by them, and so far from engaging in any Rebellion, that they have never entertained a rebellious thought; whence they humbly hope that they shall not be put to the expense of buying new cloaths." This is not a very humorous production, but at least it bears witness to the common occurrence in 1746 of the highlander's figure at the shops of snuff and tobacco-sellers.

The highlander, as he existed within living memory at many shop doors, and as he still exists at a few, was and is the survivor of many similar wooden figures as trade signs. The wooden figure of a negro or "Indian" with gilt loin-cloth and feathered head, has already been mentioned as an old tobacconist's sign. In early Georgian days a tobacconist named John Bowden, who dealt in all kinds of snuff, and also in "Aloe, Pigtail, and Wild Tobacco; with all sorts of perfumer's goods, wholesale and retail," traded at the sign of "The Highlander and Black Boy" in Threadneedle Street, London. At York, in this present year, 1914, I came upon a brightly painted wooden figure of Napoleon in full uniform and snuff-box in hand, standing at the door of a small tobacco-shop. Another class of sign or emblem was represented by the "wooden midshipman," which many of us have seen in Leadenhall Street, and which Dickens made famous in "Dombey and Son." Sometimes the wooden figure of a sailor stood outside public-houses with such signs as "The Jolly Sailor"; and a black doll was long a familiar token of the loathly shop kept by the tradesmen mysteriously known as Marine Store Dealers. Images of this kind sometimes stood at the door, or in many cases were placed on brackets or swung from the lintels.

Sir Walter Scott said that in London a Scotchman would walk half a mile farther to purchase his ounce of snuff where the sign of the Highlander announced a North Briton.

Dickens's little figure, which adorned old Sol Gills's shop, "thrust itself out above the pavement, right leg foremost," with shoe buckles and flapped waistcoat very much unlike the real thing, and "bore at its right eye the most offensively disproportionate piece of machinery." But this was only one of many "little timber midshipmen in obsolete naval uniforms, eternally employed outside the shop-doors of nautical instrument-makers in taking observations of the hackney-coaches." All have disappeared, together with the black dolls of the rag shops and many other old-time figures. A stray highlander or two, or other figure, may survive here and there; but with very few exceptions indeed, the once abundant tobacconists' signs have disappeared from our streets as completely as the emblems and tokens of other trades.

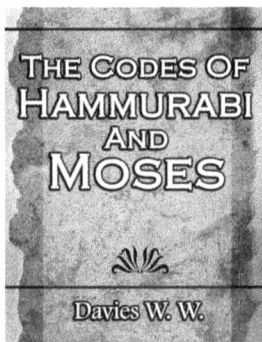

The Codes Of Hammurabi And Moses
W. W. Davies

QTY

The discovery of the Hammurabi Code is one of the greatest achievements of archaeology, and is of paramount interest, not only to the student of the Bible, but also to all those interested in ancient history...

Religion   **ISBN:** *1-59462-338-4*

Pages:132

MSRP $12.95

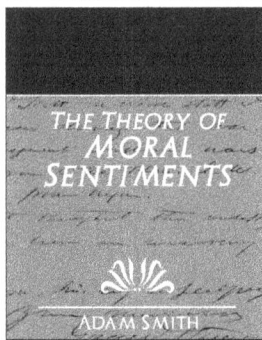

The Theory of Moral Sentiments
Adam Smith

QTY

This work from 1749. contains original theories of conscience amd moral judgment and it is the foundation for systemof morals.

Philosophy **ISBN:** *1-59462-777-0*

Pages:536

MSRP $19.95

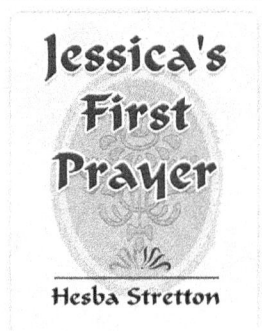

Jessica's First Prayer
Hesba Stretton

QTY

In a screened and secluded corner of one of the many railway-bridges which span the streets of London there could be seen a few years ago, from five o'clock every morning until half past eight, a tidily set-out coffee-stall, consisting of a trestle and board, upon which stood two large tin cans, with a small fire of charcoal burning under each so as to keep the coffee boiling during the early hours of the morning when the work-people were thronging into the city on their way to their daily toil...

Pages:84

Childrens   **ISBN:** *1-59462-373-2*

MSRP $9.95

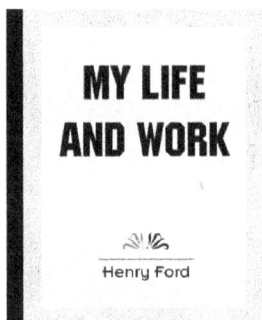

My Life and Work
Henry Ford

QTY

Henry Ford revolutionized the world with his implementation of mass production for the Model T automobile. Gain valuable business insight into his life and work with his own auto-biography... "We have only started on our development of our country we have not as yet, with all our talk of wonderful progress, done more than scratch the surface. The progress has been wonderful enough but..."

Pages:300

Biographies/   **ISBN:** *1-59462-198-5*

MSRP $21.95

The Art of Cross-Examination
Francis Wellman

I presume it is the experience of every author, after his first book is published upon an important subject, to be almost overwhelmed with a wealth of ideas and illustrations which could readily have been included in his book, and which to his own mind, at least, seem to make a second edition inevitable. Such certainly was the case with me; and when the first edition had reached its sixth impression in five months, I rejoiced to learn that it seemed to my publishers that the book had met with a sufficiently favorable reception to justify a second and considerably enlarged edition. ...

Reference   **ISBN:** *1-59462-647-2*   **Pages:412** **MSRP $19.95**

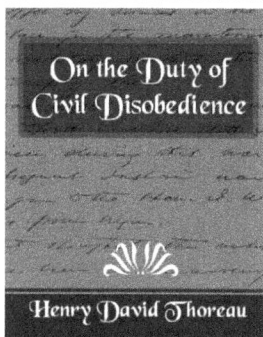

On the Duty of Civil Disobedience
Henry David Thoreau

Thoreau wrote his famous essay, On the Duty of Civil Disobedience, as a protest against an unjust but popular war and the immoral but popular institution of slave-owning. He did more than write—he declined to pay his taxes, and was hauled off to gaol in consequence. Who can say how much this refusal of his hastened the end of the war and of slavery ?

Law   **ISBN:** *1-59462-747-9*   **Pages:48** **MSRP $7.45**

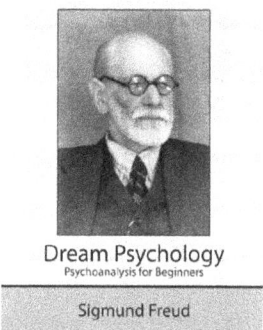

Dream Psychology Psychoanalysis for Beginners
Sigmund Freud

Sigmund Freud, born Sigismund Schlomo Freud (May 6, 1856 - September 23, 1939), was a Jewish-Austrian neurologist and psychiatrist who co-founded the psychoanalytic school of psychology. Freud is best known for his theories of the unconscious mind, especially involving the mechanism of repression; his redefinition of sexual desire as mobile and directed towards a wide variety of objects; and his therapeutic techniques, especially his understanding of transference in the therapeutic relationship and the presumed value of dreams as sources of insight into unconscious desires.

Psychology   **ISBN:** *1-59462-905-6*   **Pages:196** **MSRP $15.45**

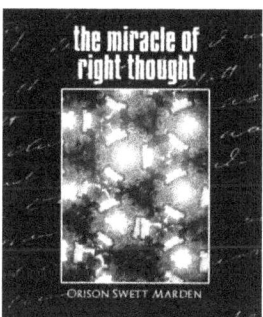

The Miracle of Right Thought
Orison Swett Marden

Believe with all of your heart that you will do what you were made to do. When the mind has once formed the habit of holding cheerful, happy, prosperous pictures, it will not be easy to form the opposite habit. It does not matter how improbable or how far away this realization may see, or how dark the prospects may be, if we visualize them as best we can, as vividly as possible, hold tenaciously to them and vigorously struggle to attain them, they will gradually become actualized, realized in the life. But a desire, a longing without endeavor, a yearning abandoned or held indifferently will vanish without realization.

Self Help   **ISBN:** *1-59462-644-8*   **Pages:360** **MSRP $25.45**

www.bookjungle.com *email: sales@bookjungle.com fax: 630-214-0564 mail: Book Jungle PO Box 2226 Champaign, IL 61825*

QTY

The Rosicrucian Cosmo-Conception Mystic Christianity *by Max Heindel*   ISBN: *1-59462-188-8*   **$38.95**
The Rosicrucian Cosmo-conception is not dogmatic, neither does it appeal to any other authority than the reason of the student. It is: not controversial, but is: sent forth in the, hope that it may help to clear...   New Age/Religion Pages 646

Abandonment To Divine Providence *by Jean-Pierre de Caussade*   ISBN: *1-59462-228-0*   **$25.95**
"The Rev. Jean Pierre de Caussade was one of the most remarkable spiritual writers of the Society of Jesus in France in the 18th Century. His death took place at Toulouse in 1751. His works have gone through many editions and have been republished...   Inspirational/Religion Pages 400

Mental Chemistry *by Charles Haanel*   ISBN: *1-59462-192-6*   **$23.95**
Mental Chemistry allows the change of material conditions by combining and appropriately utilizing the power of the mind. Much like applied chemistry creates something new and unique out of careful combinations of chemicals the mastery of mental chemistry...   New Age Pages 354

The Letters of Robert Browning and Elizabeth Barret Barrett 1845-1846 vol II   ISBN: *1-59462-193-4*   **$35.95**
by Robert Browning and Elizabeth Barrett   Biographies Pages 596

Gleanings In Genesis (volume I) *by Arthur W. Pink*   ISBN: *1-59462-130-6*   **$27.45**
Appropriately has Genesis been termed "the seed plot of the Bible" for in it we have, in germ form, almost all of the great doctrines which are afterwards fully developed in the books of Scripture which follow...   Religion/Inspirational Pages 420

The Master Key *by L. W. de Laurence*   ISBN: *1-59462-001-6*   **$30.95**
In no branch of human knowledge has there been a more lively increase of the spirit of research during the past few years than in the study of Psychology, Concentration and Mental Discipline. The requests for authentic lessons in Thought Control, Mental Discipline and...   New Age/Business Pages 422

The Lesser Key Of Solomon Goetia *by L. W. de Laurence*   ISBN: *1-59462-092-X*   **$9.95**
This translation of the first book of the "Lemegton" which is now for the first time made accessible to students of Talismanic Magic was done, after careful collation and edition, from numerous Ancient Manuscripts in Hebrew, Latin, and French...   New Age/Occult Pages 92

Rubaiyat Of Omar Khayyam *by Edward Fitzgerald*   ISBN:*1-59462-332-5*   **$13.95**
Edward Fitzgerald, whom the world has already learned, in spite of his own efforts to remain within the shadow of anonymity, to look upon as one of the rarest poets of the century, was born at Bredfield, in Suffolk, on the 31st of March, 1809. He was the third son of John Purcell...   Music Pages 172

Ancient Law *by Henry Maine*   ISBN: *1-59462-128-4*   **$29.95**
The chief object of the following pages is to indicate some of the earliest ideas of mankind, as they are reflected in Ancient Law, and to point out the relation of those ideas to modern thought.   Religion/History Pages 452

Far-Away Stories *by William J. Locke*   ISBN: *1-59462-129-2*   **$19.45**
"Good wine needs no bush, but a collection of mixed vintages does. And this book is just such a collection. Some of the stories I do not want to remain buried for ever in the museum files of dead magazine-numbers an author's not unpardonable vanity..."   Fiction Pages 272

Life of David Crockett *by David Crockett*   ISBN: *1-59462-250-7*   **$27.45**
"Colonel David Crockett was one of the most remarkable men of the times in which he lived. Born in humble life, but gifted with a strong will, an indomitable courage, and unremitting perseverance...   Biographies/New Age Pages 424

Lip-Reading *by Edward Nitchie*   ISBN: *1-59462-206-X*   **$25.95**
Edward B. Nitchie, founder of the New York School for the Hard of Hearing, now the Nitchie School of Lip-Reading, Inc, wrote "LIP-READING Principles and Practice". The development and perfecting of this meritorious work on lip-reading was an undertaking...   How-to Pages 400

A Handbook of Suggestive Therapeutics, Applied Hypnotism, Psychic Science   ISBN: *1-59462-214-0*   **$24.95**
by Henry Munro   Health/New Age/Health/Self-help Pages 376

A Doll's House: and Two Other Plays *by Henrik Ibsen*   ISBN: *1-59462-112-8*   **$19.95**
Henrik Ibsen created this classic when in revolutionary 1848 Rome. Introducing some striking concepts in playwriting for the realist genre, this play has been studied the world over.   Fiction/Classics/Plays 308

The Light of Asia *by sir Edwin Arnold*   ISBN: *1-59462-204-3*   **$13.95**
In this poetic masterpiece, Edwin Arnold describes the life and teachings of Buddha. The man who was to become known as Buddha to the world was born as Prince Gautama of India but he rejected the worldly riches and abandoned the reigns of power when...   Religion/History/Biographies Pages 170

The Complete Works of Guy de Maupassant *by Guy de Maupassant*   ISBN: *1-59462-157-8*   **$16.95**
"For days and days, nights and nights, I had dreamed of that first kiss which was to consecrate our engagement, and I knew not on what spot I should put my lips..."   Fiction/Classics Pages 240

The Art of Cross-Examination *by Francis L. Wellman*   ISBN: *1-59462-309-0*   **$26.95**
Written by a renowned trial lawyer, Wellman imparts his experience and uses case studies to explain how to use psychology to extract desired information through questioning.   How-to/Science/Reference Pages 408

Answered or Unanswered? *by Louisa Vaughan*   ISBN: *1-59462-248-5*   **$10.95**
Miracles of Faith in China   Religion Pages 112

The Edinburgh Lectures on Mental Science (1909) *by Thomas*   ISBN: *1-59462-008-3*   **$11.95**
This book contains the substance of a course of lectures recently given by the writer in the Queen Street Hail, Edinburgh. Its purpose is to indicate the Natural Principles governing the relation between Mental Action and Material Conditions...   New Age/Psychology Pages 148

Ayesha *by H. Rider Haggard*   ISBN: *1-59462-301-5*   **$24.95**
Verily and indeed it is the unexpected that happens! Probably if there was one person upon the earth from whom the Editor of this, and of a certain previous history, did not expect to hear again...   Classics Pages 380

Ayala's Angel *by Anthony Trollope*   ISBN: *1-59462-352-X*   **$29.95**
The two girls were both pretty, but Lucy who was twenty-one who supposed to be simple and comparatively unattractive, whereas Ayala was credited, as her Bombwhat romantic name might show, with poetic charm and a taste for romance. Ayala when her father died was nineteen...   Fiction Pages 484

The American Commonwealth *by James Bryce*   ISBN: *1-59462-286-8*   **$34.45**
An interpretation of American democratic political theory. It examines political mechanics and society from the perspective of Scotsman James Bryce   Politics Pages 572

Stories of the Pilgrims *by Margaret P. Pumphrey*   ISBN: *1-59462-116-0*   **$17.95**
This book explores pilgrims religious oppression in England as well as their escape to Holland and eventual crossing to America on the Mayflower, and their early days in New England...   History Pages 268

www.bookjungle.com *email: sales@bookjungle.com fax: 630-214-0564 mail: Book Jungle PO Box 2226 Champaign, IL 61825*

QTY

The Fasting Cure *by **Sinclair Upton***   ISBN: *1-59462-222-1* **$13.95**
In the Cosmopolitan Magazine for May, 1910, and in the Contemporary Review (London) for April, 1910, I published an article dealing with my experiences in fasting. I have written a great many magazine articles, but never one which attracted so much attention... New Age/Self Help/Health Pages 164

Hebrew Astrology *by **Sepharial***   ISBN: *1-59462-308-2* **$13.45**
In these days of advanced thinking it is a matter of common observation that we have left many of the old landmarks behind and that we are now pressing forward to greater heights and to a wider horizon than that which represented the mind-content of our progenitors... Astrology Pages 144

Thought Vibration or The Law of Attraction in the Thought World   ISBN: *1-59462-127-6* **$12.95**

*by **William Walker Atkinson***   *Psychology/Religion Pages 144*

Optimism *by **Helen Keller***   ISBN: *1-59462-108-X* **$15.95**
Helen Keller was blind, deaf, and mute since 19 months old, yet famously learned how to overcome these handicaps, communicate with the world, and spread her lectures promoting optimism. An inspiring read for everyone... Biographies/Inspirational Pages 84

Sara Crewe *by **Frances Burnett***   ISBN: *1-59462-360-0* **$9.45**
In the first place, Miss Minchin lived in London. Her home was a large, dull, tall one, in a large, dull square, where all the houses were alike, and all the sparrows were alike, and where all the door-knockers made the same heavy sound... Childrens/Classic Pages 88

The Autobiography of Benjamin Franklin *by **Benjamin Franklin***   ISBN: *1-59462-135-7* **$24.95**
The Autobiography of Benjamin Franklin has probably been more extensively read than any other American historical work, and no other book of its kind has had such ups and downs of fortune. Franklin lived for many years in England, where he was agent... Biographies/History Pages 332

Name	
Email	
Telephone	
Address	
City, State ZIP	

☐ **Credit Card**   ☐ **Check / Money Order**

Credit Card Number	
Expiration Date	
Signature	

Please Mail to: Book Jungle
PO Box 2226
Champaign, IL 61825
or Fax to: 630-214-0564

ORDERING INFORMATION

web*: www.bookjungle.com*
email*: sales@bookjungle.com*
fax*: 630-214-0564*
mail*: Book Jungle PO Box 2226 Champaign, IL 61825*
or PayPal *to sales@bookjungle.com*

Please contact us for bulk discounts

DIRECT-ORDER TERMS

**20% Discount if You Order
Two or More Books**
Free Domestic Shipping!
Accepted: Master Card, Visa,
Discover, American Express

www.ingramcontent.com/pod-product-compliance
Lightning Source LLC
Chambersburg PA
CBHW081229090426
42738CB00016B/3235

* 9 7 8 1 4 3 8 5 0 6 8 9 0 *